ADVANCE PRAISE FOR

INVISIBLE SLAVES:
The Victims and Perpetrators
of Modern-Day Slavery

This is a deeply moving book. Factual and calm, Kurt Hauser issues a carefully documented, urgent wake-up call. Slavery remains shockingly pervasive around the world in the 21st century, even in Western countries. With this book, Hauser helps slavery's invisible victims to be heard.

> – *Ayaan Hirsi Ali, Research Fellow at the Hoover Institution, Stanford University, and founder of the AHA Foundation*

Invisible Slaves recounts in readable prose and riveting detail the pervasiveness of contemporary slavery, found beyond just developing lands in our own Facebook world. This *tour d'horizon* blends numerical data with tragic vignettes of individuals swallowed up in shadowy and wicked enslavement. By writing this unflinching account Kurt Hauser opens our consciousness, our minds, and our hearts to a present-day evil too often ignored.

> – *Thomas H. Henriksen, Senior Fellow at the Hoover Institution*

INVISIBLE SLAVES

The Victims and Perpetrators of Modern-Day Slavery

INVISIBLE SLAVES

The Victims and Perpetrators of Modern-Day Slavery

W. Kurt Hauser

HOOVER INSTITUTION PRESS
Stanford University   Stanford, California

With its eminent scholars and world-renowned library and archives, the Hoover Institution seeks to improve the human condition by advancing ideas that promote economic opportunity and prosperity, while securing and safeguarding peace for America and all mankind. The views expressed in its publications are entirely those of the authors and do not necessarily reflect the views of the staff, officers, or Board of Overseers of the Hoover Institution.

www.hoover.org

Hoover Institution Press Publication No. 684

Hoover Institution at Leland Stanford Junior University,
Stanford, California 94305-6003

First printing 2017

24 23 22 21 20 19 18 17   8 7 6 5 4 3 2 1

Manufactured in the United States of America

The paper used in this publication meets the minimum requirements of
the American National Standard for Information Sciences—Permanence
of Paper for Printed Library Materials, ANSI/NISO Z39.48-1992. ∞

Cataloging-in-Publication Data is available from the Library of Congress.
ISBN 978-0-8179-2105-7 (pbk. : alk. paper)
ISBN 978-0-8179-2106-4 (epub)
ISBN 978-0-8179-2107-1 (mobi)
ISBN 978-0-8179-2108-8 (PDF)

To Julie

Contents

Preface

MATUL WAS 17 YEARS OLD, working as a housekeeper in her native Indonesia, when a cousin of her employers offered her a job in America. Matul jumped at the opportunity: "Who doesn't want to come to the U.S.? It seemed like a great opportunity at the time."

As soon as she arrived at the airport in the United States, her new "employer" confiscated her passport. Over the next two years, Matul was forced to work seven days a week with no pay. Her employers beat her when she protested and told her that, because she lacked a passport, she would be arrested and raped in prison if she ever tried to escape. Matul had become an invisible slave.

"She was threatening me, saying that if I ran away, the police would arrest me because I didn't have my passport, and that I'd be thrown in jail where I'd be raped," said Matul, who didn't speak any English at the time.

Finally, after years of suffering and managing to cobble together enough English, Matul was able to slip a note to a nanny working at a nearby home: "Please help me."[1]

Matul is a modern-day slave.

Matul was not a faceless victim on a faraway shore. She had arrived in the United States legally and was subjected to these crimes in the middle of one of America's most affluent neighborhoods in Southern California. According to the Walk Free Foundation's 2016 Global Slavery Index, Matul was just one of an estimated 57,700 people subjected to slavery in the United States.[2]

This book's purpose is simple: to bring awareness to the global problem of modern-day slavery. The legacy of slavery haunts modern-day

Western Civilization and especially the United States. Indeed, critics of the West cite slavery among the many evils spawned by Western Civilization in general and the United States in particular. But nothing could be further from the truth. Slavery existed before the discovery of the New World and before the origins of Western Civilization. The abolition movement is Western in origin and sprung out of the enlightenment in Europe. Great Britain and the United States were the first countries to ban the trade in slaves and the West led the globe in enacting laws prohibiting the institution of slavery. Yet slavery continues to exist in virtually every country of the world. Thus, slavery is not a problem of the past, but a present-day scourge.

Today, according to the Walk Free Foundation's Global Slavery Index, a staggering 45.8 million people in the world live under the crushing bonds of slavery: forced, coerced, tricked, or otherwise compelled against their wills to perform involuntary acts, sexual or otherwise, without just remuneration. Slavery generates revenue in excess of $150 billion annually according to the International Labour Organization, a United Nations agency. In terms of global criminal activity, human trafficking ranks second only to the illicit drug trade in annual dollar revenue, according to the United Nations Office on Drugs and Crime.

Modern day slavery estimated by **gender:**
55% women and girls; 45% men and boys [3]

Understanding where slavery came from—and how deeply the institution is woven into the fabric of human history—is vital to understanding the differing contexts in which slavery operates around the world today. This book begins with a brief overview of slavery's history and a discussion of its different meanings and practicalities over time before delving into a region-by-region discussion of modern-day slavery. It also addresses the responses that various countries are making to combat slavery. Many sources exist (and are cited heavily within this book) that take a close look at the extent of slavery around the world. It is not the intent of this book to cover all countries; instead, this work will highlight what are deemed to be the most problematic and indicative cases in order to impress upon the reader the urgency and ubiquity of the global problem.

Modern day slavery estimated by **profits:**
Forced **sexual** exploitation: **$99 billion**
Forced **labor** exploitation: **$51 billion** [4]

Throughout the book are first-hand stories of modern-day slaves and trafficking, included to personalize the issue and remind the reader that as many as 46 million human beings will wake up today to a life of forced labor, violence, sexual assault, and dehumanization under the yoke of slavery.

Slavery is one of humankind's oldest institutions, a practice that dates back over 12,000 years to the earliest recorded history. Slavery, however, is not a bygone problem. Slavery is a twenty-first century problem. It is an American problem, a Western problem, an Eastern problem, it is a world problem. It is a global problem and, as such, it will require a global solution. A major part of the solution is an acknowledgement and awareness that slavery exists today in all reaches of the globe.

It is possible, indeed likely, that the clothes and shoes that you wear, the mobile phone and computer you use, the chocolate that you eat, the diamonds, gold, and jewelry that you wear, the coffee that you drink, and the food you eat have at some point been touched by the hands of slaves.

This book provides an overview of the powerful, overarching impact that slavery has had on the development of the modern world. The great abolitionist William Wilberforce said it best: "You may choose to look the other way, but you can never say you did not know." Hopefully, this book will encourage free people to rethink their lives and reorder their choices in order to be a force for freedom around the world.

CHAPTER ONE
An Ancient Institution

WAR AND RELIGION. TRADE AND COMMERCE. DRAWING AND PAINTING. A few practices and institutions date to the oldest records of the human experience. With the advent of agriculture and animal husbandry at the end of the last Ice Age, about 10,000 BC, another ancient institution arose: slavery. Slavery wove itself into the fabric of virtually every society, culture, and civilization.

Slavery was ubiquitous in Asia, India, Europe, China, the Middle East, Africa, and the pre-colonial Americas as far back as the records of each region can be traced. The practice and spread of slavery catalyzed the regionalization, and eventually the globalization, of the world's labor markets. For four centuries, slavery was the world's largest commerce. From AD 1500 to 1900, at least 26 million Sub-Saharan Africans were captured and sold into slavery: upwards of twelve million Sub-Saharan Africans were transported to the New World, six million to the Middle East and Islamic Mediterranean region, and eight million enslaved and retained within Africa.[1] Millions of other humans were subjected to slavery in the near and far east as Islam spread to these regions and conflicts occurred between the Ottoman Empire, Russia, the Tartars, and the Mongols.

Slavery has never been a standalone industry. Indeed, the Atlantic and Middle Eastern slave trades formed the basis for a "triangle of trade" that jumpstarted the world economy and, at its peak, dwarfed today's globalization of world trade in both magnitude and scope. In this "triangle of trade," Europeans shipped their products to Africa, the Africans sold their captives to the Europeans for transport and sale to

1

the plantations of the New World, and New World plantation owners shipped their commodities back across the Atlantic to the Europeans. Similar transactions involving slaves, commodities and finished goods took place between and among the Middle East, Eurasia, Asia and other areas of the globe. The demand for slaves, and the economic system that would develop to support it, provided the infrastructure for 400 years of international commerce.

The demographic impact of the Atlantic slave trade was enormous. In the 300 years after the "discovery" of the New World in 1492, five African slaves were transported to the Americas for every one European settler. As late as 1840, the annual number of African slaves coming to the Americas exceeded the number of Europeans. However, of the approximate 9.5 to 11 million African slaves transported to the New World during the Atlantic slave trade, less than 5 percent of those African slaves came to what would eventually be the United States. Approximately 80 percent came to Brazil and the Caribbean Islands, and the remainder was distributed throughout Latin and South America. An equal if not greater number of black African slaves were sold into the markets of the Middle East, Eurasia, and Asia over a longer period of time.

Slavery, at its root, is an economic phenomenon. Its origin was driven by the demand for (and eventual division of) labor following the development of agriculture. The practice of slavery over time has ebbed and flowed with the health and scope of the world economy—levels of trade, commerce, and industry, and the resulting impact on demands for labor worldwide. In Western Civilization, the practice reached its zenith during the economically prosperous era of ancient Greece (fifth century BC) and the Roman Empire that followed. Slavery also flourished in other powerful ancient civilizations, including India, China, Korea, Egypt, Asia, Africa, and the Americas.

Nearly all of the world's major religions endorsed and accepted slavery, including Judaism, Buddhism, Hinduism, Christianity, Islam, paganism, and animism. The ancient codes and laws of antiquity, including the Bible, Talmud, and Quran, direct many pages to the recognition, acceptance and regulation of slavery.[2] The surviving primary documents of both Western and Eastern Civilizations, derived from oral traditions of the prehistoric past, all reference slavery. For instance, in Genesis Chapter 9, Noah curses his grandson Canaan (son of Ham) and makes him a "servant of servants" in one of many references to slavery in the Old Testament. There are numerous references in both the *Iliad* and the *Odyssey* to both male and female slaves. The Phoenicians and Taphians are mentioned as slave traders in Homer's *Iliad* and *Odyssey*. Slavery is also mentioned repeatedly in the Code of Hammurabi, the Hebrew Bible, the Gortyn Code of Ancient Greece, and India's Rigveda. Among the oldest records of slavery are those passed down from Ancient Egypt. Texts from the reign of the Pharaoh Ramses II (1291–1224 BC) allude to slave labor; however, Hebrew enslavement in Egypt is not confirmed in Egyptian texts but rather in the Bible. In his writings in Deuteronomy, Moses instructed the Israelites to "remember that thou wast a servant in the land of Egypt."[3] From ancient Babylon, Assyria, Syria, Palestine to ancient China, India, and the entirety of the Americas, the written records of humanity's ancient past demonstrate that slavery existed, at one time or another, in virtually every human society.

An Ancient Debate and Slavery's Evolution

ARISTOTLE (384–322 BC) AND PLATO (ca. 428–424 BC), the great Greek philosophers, debated whether slavery was part of nature, the natural order of the universe, or the creation of man. If slavery was as old as humankind, then was the slave created by the laws of man, of nature, or of God?

In *Politics*, Aristotle notes that the master-slave relationship appeared as natural as the husband-wife and father-child relationship, and that humanity is divided between master and slave. However, Aristotle frames the debate by stating that "the rule of a master over slaves is contrary to nature, and ... the distinction between slave and freeman exists by law only, and not by nature; and being an interference with nature is therefore unjust."[4]

> The master is only the master of the slave; he does not belong to him, whereas the slave is not only the slave of his master but wholly belongs to him. Hence we see what is the nature and office of a slave; he who is by nature not his own but another's man, is by nature a slave; and he may be said to be another's man who, being a human being, is also a possession.[5]

> But is there any one thus intended by nature to be a slave, and for whom such a condition is expedient and right, or rather is not all slavery a violation of nature?

> There is no difficulty in answering this question, on grounds both of reason and of fact. For that some should rule and others be ruled is a thing not only necessary, but expedient; from the hour of their birth, some are marked out for subjection, others for rule.[6]

Therefore, slaves are of nature because they are necessary and expedient.

Some scholars seem to reconcile this contradiction within Aristotle by suggesting that existing laws, customs, and traditions confirm the natural origin of slaves. Masters, by nature, are not meant to become slaves (as captives in war), whereby those naturally born to be slaves are not meant to be masters. Prisoners of war were not natural slaves, but through misfortune became slaves by law. Aristotle also separates the master from the slave by attributing virtue, a soul, and character to the master and not to the slave.

Plato is less expansive on the origin of slaves but rationalizes their existence by explaining that they lack the ability to reason, therefore they needed masters to rule their lives. In his ideal state as described in *Republic*, slaves are an integral part of the society. In Plato's view, justice consists of the superior ruling over the inferior and having more power than the inferior among humans as well as among animals.

Regardless of the philosophers' arguments about slavery as to its origin, virtually all slave societies had statutes and codes regarding the just treatment of slaves and their individual manumission.

Although Aristotle rationalized the natural origin of slavery, he also believed in the incentive of manumission: the master granting his slave eventual freedom in exchange for good behavior and productive work. According to Aristotle, the prospects of manumission were both "just and expedient" as rationalized above. Manumission could be earned by the slave through a process whereby the slave bought his or her freedom, or manumission could be granted as a gift by the master.

David Livingstone (1813–1873), the nineteenth-century British explorer, believed that slavery was a natural part of human development. But Livingstone was horrified by the slavery he witnessed in his missionary work in Africa. He was an ardent proponent for the elimination of slavery in Africa. In his *Journals*, Livingstone writes:

> We may compare cannibalism to the stone age, and the times of slavery to the iron and bronze epochs—slavery is as natural a step in human development as from bronze to iron.
>
> …The monuments of Egypt show that this curse has venerable antiquity.[7]

Slavery thus began as humans transitioned from hunters and gatherers and nomadic tribes following their food source to the cultivation of crops and the domestication of livestock. Captives in war and skirmishes could then be put to work and produce more than they consumed. Prior to the advent of agriculture, a captive would have been a burden on the group and either killed, held for sacrifice, or traded to the opposing tribe for a captive they may have had of their own tribe.

As humans began to organize themselves around settlements, captives in war could be put to work not only in agriculture but also in mining, land and swamp clearing, building and construction, and various menial tasks. These small tribal settlements gave way to larger lineage groups, and then organizations of city-states, states, empires, and the nation-state. Slavery was an important part in this evolution of political systems.

Slaves fulfilled three main functions: social (harems, concubines, eunuchs), political (military, bureaucrats, administrators), and economic (modes of production). In many African cultures, slaves could also be counted as members of the tribe and could be assimilated into the family or clan. This enhanced the stature of the family. Land was owned by the tribe or central government. Wealth was attained by owning slaves not land. However, there was a constant need to replenish slaves due to manumission, assimilation, death, or escape.

In many societies slaves were poets, writers, musicians, and handicraft workers in addition to being laborers. It was not uncommon for slaves to become the wives of their masters. Many Islamic states used slaves in their military. Non-Muslim prisoners of war were trained as warriors, converted to Islam, and conscripted to the military. In Egypt, these slave soldiers were called Mamluks and eventually ruled the country for some three hundred years, beginning in the middle of the thirteenth century.

The war captive who became a slave was also alien to the new tribe or political organization, and considered a foreigner and outsider. In several societies, the word for slave meant a person of a foreign country, one who was most likely taken as a captive in war or kidnapping. Among the ancient Greek states, captives taken in war were of the same ethnicity but were of another country. This was also true of the slaves held among the Hebrews and Israelites. It was not until the fifteenth century that race became associated with slavery in the Western world. Arabs may have preempted the New World in viewing slavery as a matter of race because of their longer history of black slave trading along the various trade routes from Sub-Saharan Africa to North Africa, the Middle East and Asia. As early as the ninth century, and possibly before, Arab traders spreading the Islamic faith carried black Africans to North Africa and the Mediterranean as slaves. The Arab word for slave, *abid*, increasingly became associated with black Africans.

Racism can be characterized as one group of people feeling superior to another based on ethnic, tribal, kinship, or perceived racial differences. Slavery was often justified in the Christian world because it was thought to be sanctioned in the Old Testament. Some slavers claimed that Noah cursed his son Ham for an indiscretion and as punishment condemned his son, Canaan, to both blackness and slavery. A divine sanction to slavery, "The Curse of Ham," evolved from this erroneous interpretation of the Bible. According to this myth, blacks were descendants of Ham's son and their enslavement was justified. The white rulers of South Africa during the apartheid years of 1948–1994 used "The Curse of Ham" to justify their segregationist and racial policies. This tale was used by many Christians as justification for the enslavement or mistreatment of blacks. Scholars continue to explore the origin and linkage of blackness, darkness, servitude, slavery, and race.

The words of Judge Roger B. Taney, in delivering the opinion of the Supreme Court in the *Dred Scott* decision in 1857, illustrate how racism has "colored" the minds of even the most educated:

> They [slaves] had for more than a century before been regarded as beings of an inferior order, and altogether unfit to associate with the white race either in social or political relations, and so far inferior that they had no rights which the white man was bound to respect, and that the negro might justly and lawfully be reduced to slavery for his benefit.[8]

Thus, it was thought to be to the Negro's benefit to be enslaved!

While slavery has been legally banned in all countries, racism persists. In the centuries that followed the fall of the Roman Empire, roughly the sixth century to the fourteenth century, much of the former Empire sank into a prolonged depression referred to by many as the Dark Ages. This period included the rise of Vandal and barbarian tribes that ravaged much of Europe, the dearth of Latin literature and historical writing, periods of plague and disease, and lack of material cultural accomplishment. Trade and commerce declined compared to the Roman period. Most of Northern Europe devolved into feudalism, a social and economic system in which the Crown granted land to nobility in exchange for military service. In this system, slavery was replaced by serfdom, in which peasants—or serfs—worked their lord's land and gave him a share of what they produced in exchange for protection. However, slavery did not disappear altogether; captives in war were often either kept as slaves or sold into slavery. The Middle Ages transitioned into the Italian Renaissance in the fourteenth century, and the so-called Dark Ages, which extinguished the "light of Rome," faded into history.

At the same time, on the periphery of Europe, in the Iberian Peninsula to the west, the Byzantine Empire to the east, and in North Africa to the south, the spread of Islam spurred trade and commerce and preserved the need for slave labor. As Islam advanced from Arabia in the seventh and eighth centuries across North Africa to the west, the Middle East and Asia Minor to the north, and East Africa to the south, a rich harvest in slaves occurred in the conquered lands. Debtor, criminal, and hereditary slavery was allowed under the religious laws of Islam. However, the enslavement of fellow Muslims was forbidden. But from time immemorial, that which is prohibited by law or religion is often practiced in real life. The enslavement of prisoners of war—infidels—was encouraged and often these included Muslims.

Beyond the eighth century, the source of slaves was manifold. The Muslims moved into Eastern Europe and Asia, and their adversaries were captured and enslaved. At the same time, the Tatars of Asia were moving west and taking their captives back home toward the east.

The constant warring between Christians and Muslims provided a

Slave Coffle, Central Africa, 1861

consistent source of slaves for both sides. Slaves acquired by the Muslims were kept by the invading marauders as domestic servants or concubines, impounded into the military, or sold on the slave markets of Istanbul, Algiers, or Lisbon. War captives of the Christians were also sold on the slave markets, retained as domestic servants, or put to use in agriculture, mining, and menial work. The North African Barbary pirates in the eighteenth century captured and sold European and American maritime sailors on the slave markets of Algiers.

Finally, the Berbers, a North African ethnic group, and Arabs developed a slave trade in Africa enslaving black Africans. The trade had three geographic routes. One route was in East Africa, where Africans captured or acquired by trade or barter were shipped to the Middle East and Asia through the Indian Ocean. The second route involved the transporting of Africans out of the Eastern Sudan and then travelling by caravan down the Nile Valley to Egypt, and from there to Mediterranean destinations. The third route was the sub-Saharan trade routes from West Africa to the Mediterranean coast of North Africa.

Arabs and Berbers exploring central and western Africa in the Middle

Ages observed an active slave trade among sub-Sahara Africans. This history of slavery in Africa is discussed in greater depth later in this book. Suffice to say that slavery in Africa by Africans can be traced back to the earliest of times.

After Columbus's voyage to the Americas in 1492, native crops in the New World were introduced to Europe, Africa, and other areas of the Old World. These crops eventually gave rise to plantation farming in Africa and the need for slave labor. These crops included maize (corn), wild rice, barley, sunflower, peanut, bean, long-staple and upland cotton, manioc (yucca, cassava), potato, sweet potato, tomato, guava, papaya, pineapple, squash, cocoa, tobacco, and rubber, among others. Indeed, once New World crops were introduced to Africa, there were eventually, in the latter part of the nineteenth century, more African slaves held by Africans than there were African slaves in the Americas.[9]

While the above developments were taking place in Europe, the Middle East, and Africa, slavery was flowing and ebbing in all the other societies, cultures and civilizations of the world. This book will touch upon the historic context of these areas when addressing modern-day slavery in the region-by-region review.

The discovery of the New World in the fifteenth century brought forth the first globalization of world trade and a new demand for labor to work the fields and mines of the Caribbean and the Americas.

The Abolitionist Movement

UP TO THE NINETEENTH CENTURY, slavery was an accepted condition of the legal and social structure of every civilization. It was not until the eighteenth century that a lasting abolitionist movement began to unfold, a slowly rising level of protest against slavery that has carried to the present day. The Hebrew Bible and other ancient texts reference manumission, the day of Jubilee, and other protections for slaves, and in several societies slaves could buy their freedom. There are references in history to slaves being freed as when Cyrus the Great conquered Babylon in

539 BC and freed all the slaves. In the early sixteenth century, Bartolome de las Casas (1484–1566), a social reformer and Dominican friar, advocated against the enslavement and torture of Native Americans in the West Indies. He influenced King Charles I of Spain (Emperor Charles V) to pass the New Laws in 1542 to abolish slavery in Spain's New World colonies. This law was not enforced, as Spain had little control over its overseas possessions. Thus, it was not until 1772 that the first modern and effective legislative measure against slavery was recorded. In that year, Lord Mansfield declared that fugitive slaves would become free upon entering Great Britain. The movement to abolish slavery, known as abolitionism, sprung from the Enlightenment, which was a European intellectual revolution of the late seventeenth century and early eighteenth century. The Enlightenment promoted ideas of individual freedom, liberty, reason, and tolerance as contrasted to the absolute rule and abuses of the church (Roman Catholic Church) and state (Monarchy). The institution of slavery was contrary to the philosophical ideas espoused by the Enlightenment. In the mid-seventeenth century in England, a Christian religious group arose that became known as Quakers, or Society of Friends. This group became one of the first to protest against slavery. By the mid-eighteenth century the Quakers' protestations were having an impact in both Great Britain and the United States. The influence of this group along with other religious organizations culminated in Great Britain abolishing the slave trade within its Empire in 1808 and abolishing slavery in all of its colonies in 1834, a mandate that was fully phased in by 1838. The United States also banned the slave trade in 1808. In 1865, the Thirteenth Amendment to the United States Constitution abolished slavery in the United States. In 1888, Brazil became the last country in the Americas to abolish slavery. The last countries to formerly abolish slavery, in name if not in practice, were Saudi Arabia and Yemen in 1962, Mauritania in 1980, and Niger in 2004.

An Evolving Definition of Slavery

SCHOLARS HAVE, FROM THE EARLIEST of times, sought to define a slave. *Webster's New Universal Unabridged Dictionary* defines a slave as

> a bond servant divested of all freedom and personal rights; a human being who is owned by and wholly subject to the will of another, as by capture, purchase, or birth; one who has lost the power to resist; drudge to work; to labor at hard, menial or unpleasant work.[10]

A bond servant is an Old English term and refers to a serf or slave or a captive. The New Testament book of I Corinthians uses the phrase "whether we be bond or free," which suggests that bond is the opposite of free.[11] Bondage is "slavery or involuntary servitude; restraint of a person's liberty by compulsion; imprisonment; captivity; serfdom."[12]

However, like the institution itself, slavery's definition has changed greatly. Understanding this evolution is more than a semantic exercise. The shifting definition of slavery sheds historic light on the changing nature of the institution over time.

In the third century BC, Aristotle wrote that "tools can be divided into animate and inanimate... So a piece of property is, similarly, a tool needed to live; 'property' is a collection of such tools, and a slave is an animate piece of property."

> It will be clear from these facts what the nature and the functions of a slave are.
>
> A human being who by nature does not belong to himself but to another person—such a one is by nature a slave.
>
> A human being belongs to another when he is a piece of property as well as being human.
>
> A piece of property is a tool which is used to assist some activity, and which has a separate existence of its own.[13]

The Byzantine Emperor Justinian I issued a set of laws between AD 529 and 534 that codified ancient Roman laws. These laws are entitled *Corpus Juris Civilis*. In them are numerous references to slavery, including definitions:

1. Slavery is an institution of the common law of peoples (ius gentium) by which a person is put into ownership (dominium) of somebody else, contrary to the natural order.

2. Slaves (servi) are so called because commanders generally sell the people they capture and thereby save (servare) them instead of killing them.

3. The word for property in slaves (mancipia) is derived from the fact that they are captured from the enemy by force of arms (manu capiantur).[14]

When the Constitution of the United States was amended to abolish slavery in 1865, it marked a pivotal shift in the global abolitionist movement. However, the Thirteenth Amendment does not define slavery other than to reference involuntary servitude:

Neither slavery nor involuntary servitude, except as a punishment for crime whereof the party shall have been duly convicted, shall exist within the United States, or any place subject to their jurisdiction.[15]

The League of Nations held a Slavery Convention in 1926. The League defined slavery as "the status or condition of a person over whom any or all of the powers attaching to the right of ownership are exercised."[16] The Convention also defined the slave trade as including "all acts involved in the capture, acquisition or disposal of a person with intent to reduce him to slavery; all acts involved in the acquisition of a slave with a view to selling or exchanging him; all acts of disposal by sale or exchange of a slave acquired with a view to being sold or exchanged, and in general, every act of trade or transport in slaves."[17]

The United Nations' 1956 Supplementary Convention on the Abolition of Slavery, the Slave Trade, and Institutions and Practices Similar to Slavery expanded the definition of slavery contained in Article 1 of the League of Nation's Slavery Convention of 1926 to include:

a. Debt bondage, that is to say, the status or condition arising from a pledge by a debtor of his personal services or of those of a person under his control as security for a debt, if the value of those services as reasonably assessed is not applied towards the liquidation of the debt or the length and nature of those services are not respectively limited and defined;

b. Serfdom, that is to say, the condition or status of a tenant who is by law, custom or agreement bound to live and labour on land belonging to another person and to render some determinate service to such other person, whether for reward or not, and is not free to change his status;

c. Any institution or practice whereby:

   i. A woman, without the right to refuse, is promised or given in marriage on payment of a consideration in money or in kind to her parents, guardian, family or other person or group; or

   ii. The husband of a woman, his family, or his clan, has the right to transfer her to another person for value received or otherwise; or

   iii. A woman on the death of her husband is liable to be inherited by another person;

d. Any institution or practice whereby a child or young person under the age of 18 years, is delivered by either or both of his natural parents or by his guardian to another person, whether for reward or not, with a view to the exploitation of the child or young person or of his labour.[18]

To expand on the above reference to debtor slavery, it is primarily practiced in the poorer and more impoverished countries in Asia and Africa. Upwards of 15 to 20 million people are victims of debt bondage.[19] This is also one of the oldest forms of slavery. Debt bondage is referenced in the Homeric poems, the Code of Hammurabi, and the Old Testament. Typically, a person will be subject to debt bondage for the non-payment of a loan when it is due. The person becomes the property of the creditor until the loan is paid. In practice, the debtor is paid an insufficient amount for his services and cannot repay the loan, and the interest charged by the master actually increases the size of the loan. The obligation is passed from one generation to the next, thus enslaving the family's offspring.

Another form of debt bondage is the pledge of work for the offer of a loan. In return for the loan, the debtor agrees to work for the creditor. The need for the loan can vary from medical emergency, dowry for a marriage, caring for a sick child, a gift for a holiday, the repayment of another loan, funeral expenses, etc. Because of the typically impoverished nature of the borrower, these loans are generally not for the purchase of land, cars, or homes. The debtor becomes the chattel property of the creditor, as collateral for the loan, and all the definitions of classical slavery are met. The debtor is subject to harsh working conditions, physical violence or the threat thereof, beatings and the dehumanizing treatment typical of chattel slavery. The debtor slave must repay the creditor (master) for the food and shelter that is provided. The slave is subject to mental, physical, and sexual abuse. To prevent the slave's escape, he or she is locked up at night and sometimes physically restrained with chains. Almost always, the debtor's passport is confiscated by the creditor. As with the non-payment of a debt, this form of debtor slavery can be passed from one generation to the next.

The continuing debate around the definition of slavery is driven by a solemn but necessary fact: slavery in the world—from most impoverished countries to the most developed leaders—is alive and well today.

The International Labour Organization defines forced labor as follows:

> Forced labour is the term used by the international community to denote situations in which persons involved—women and men, girls and boys—are made to work against their free will, coerced by their recruiter or employer, for example through violence or threats of violence, or by more subtle means such as accumulated debt, retention of identity papers or threats of denunciation to immigration authorities. Such situations can also amount to human trafficking or slavery-like practices, which are similar though not identical terms in a legal sense. International law stipulates that exacting forced labour is a crime, and should be punishable through penalties which reflect the gravity of the offence. Most countries outlaw forced labour, human trafficking and slavery-like practices in their national legislation, but successful prosecutions of offenders sadly remain few and far between.[20]

In the United States, the Victims of Trafficking and Violence Protection Act of 2000, also known as the Trafficking Victims Protection Act (TVPA), and its various reauthorizations, equates human trafficking with modern-day slavery, defining "severe forms of trafficking" as:

a. Sex trafficking in which a commercial sex act is induced by force, fraud, or coercion, or in which the person induced to perform such an act has not attained 18 years of age; or

b. The recruitment, harboring, transportation, provision, or obtaining of a person for labor or services, through the use of force, fraud, or coercion for the purpose of subjection to involuntary servitude, peonage, debt bondage, or slavery. A victim need not be physically transported from one location to another in order for the crime to fall within these definitions.[21]

Thus, the twenty-first century definition of slavery is human trafficking.

While slavery's practical definition has varied across times and cultures, classifying a "slave" as property has been a common tenet of most conventional definitions of the word. The idea of a slave as being property captures, in a broad stroke, the master-slave relationship as a relationship between the owner and the owned.

Chattel slavery is the treatment of a human being as if he or she is an article of personal or movable property (as distinct from real property). A slave, as chattel property, can be bought, sold, lent, gifted, hypothecated, inherited, or otherwise treated as the equivalent of property. A chattel slave can be treated like and has the same rights as a cow, horse, goat or pig as far as the owner is concerned. Indeed, the word chattel comes from the French word for cattle. The chattel principle was a key concept underpinning the institution of slavery:

> The being of slavery, its soul and its body, lives and moves in the chattel principle, the property principle, the bill of sale principle; the cart-whip, starvation, and nakedness are its inevitable consequences....You cannot constitute slavery without the chattel principle—and with the chattel principle you cannot save it from these results. Talk not about kind and Christian masters. They are not masters of the system. The system is master of them...[22]

However, as sociologist Orlando Patterson points out in *Slavery and Social Death*, more complex social and economic relationships require a more nuanced approach. These relationships include some type of "sale" of humans in nontraditional arrangements, like the situations of indentured servants, peons, debt-bondsmen, and the exchanging of wives-to-be for a dowry in many cultures. Yet one might not consider these groupings of people to be slaves under the strict meaning of the word prior to the 1956 United Nation's enhanced articles of definitions.

Patterson postulates that additional definitions must be applied to slavery to incorporate the full meaning of the condition. One additional definition is that the slave condition is a substitute for death (for example, when the prisoner is taken in battle). More importantly, Patterson believes that the distinguishing characteristics of slavery, in addition to the slave's status as mere property, are violence, natal alienation, and dishonor.

Violence and the threat of violence are key elements of the relationship between master and slave. Put simply, the use of violence has been the most effective tool used by masters to bend the behavior of slaves to the master's will. There is much empirical evidence from the fifteenth century to the current time about the use of violence to subjugate, coerce, and punish slaves. Such evidence in earlier periods and in antiquity is anecdotal because of the paucity of surviving historical records and illiteracy of most slaves, although there are references to the general sufferings of slaves in the Bible and other ancient works.

The third characteristic of slavery, according to Patterson, beyond ownership and violence, is that of "natal alienation." Natal alienation is the severing of all ties and connections to the genetic family, the "loss of ties of birth in both ascending and descending generations."[23] Perhaps the clearest narrative of natal alienation comes from the writings of Frederick Douglass (1817–1895),[24] the son of a white slave master and a black slave woman, who escaped slavery to become an articulate spokesman for abolition in America:

> Nor, indeed, can I impart much knowledge concerning my parents. Genealogical trees do not flourish among slaves....The practice of separating children from their mothers, and hiring the latter out at distances too great to admit of their meeting, except at long intervals, is a marked feature of the cruelty and barbarity of the slave system. But it is in harmony with the grand aim of slavery, which, always and everywhere, is to re-

duce man to a level with the brute. It is a successful method of obliterating from the mind and heart of the slave, all just ideas of the sacredness of the family, as an institution....Slavery does away with fathers, as it does away with families. Slavery has no use for either fathers or families, and its laws do not recognize their existence in the social arrangements of the plantation.... By far the larger part of the slaves know as little of their ages as horses know of theirs, and it is the wish of most masters within my knowledge to keep their slaves thus ignorant.[25]

From the beginning of time, slaves taken as captives in war or raids lost all contact with their ancestors. This was also potentially true for generations born to the enslaved, since the master could sell off parts of the family. The fear of and lack of control over family breakups played a role in the psychology of slaves. Former slave Harriet A. Jacobs (1813–1897) describes this condition in her autobiography, *Incidents in the Life of a Slave Girl*:

This poor creature had witnessed the sale of her children, and seen them carried off to parts unknown, without any hopes of ever hearing from them again.

Husbands were torn from wives, parents from children, never to look upon each other again this side the grave.[26]

Mende Nazer, a young girl mentioned later in this book who was captured by slave raiders in the southern Sudan and sold into a slave market, expresses this sense of natal separation.

I was overcome with grief. But, more than anything, I was filled with an intense loneliness. I had been enfolded with love and kindness all my life. Now I was completely and utterly alone.[27]

Shyima El-Sayed Hassan, also mentioned later in this book, was sold into slavery at age eight in Egypt. She also expresses this sense of natal separation when she realizes that her mother has sold her to pay off her sister's debt.

> Then my mother began to talk about me as if I were nothing more than a piece of furniture, a commodity. How could she talk about me in this callous manner? Didn't she love me anymore? A black hole formed in the core of my being as I realized I was going to have to leave my mother, my siblings, my home, my life. I had rarely been outside of my neighborhood and had certainly never been around strangers this far from home. I was confused and began to cry hard enough to shake my whole body.[28]

Slave narratives are limited, either because they have not survived or because most slaves were, and many are today, illiterate. However, one that has survived relates to the sale of captives taken by pirates. For centuries, the North African Barbary states of Tunisia, Morocco, and Algiers raided the Mediterranean and the Atlantic coast as far north as the North Sea. In 1631 Barbary pirates raided Ireland and carried away over 100 captives to be transported back to North Africa and sold on the slave market in Algiers. A priest provides this eye-witness account of natal alienation and the fate of the captives:

> It was a piteous sight to see them exposed for sale at Algiers, for then they parted the wife from the husband, and the father from the child; then, say I, they sell the husband here, and the wife there, tearing from her arms a daughter whom she cannot hope to see ever again.[29]

The narratives of modern-day slaves, such as those cited earlier from the Sudan and Egypt, and those that follow in the later chapters of this book, suggest that natal alienation or separation is a common condition of modern-day slavery.

A final characteristic of the practice of slavery, in addition to viewing slaves as property, the violence intrinsic to the system, and natal alienation, is a sense of dishonor. Dishonor appears to be a natural condition of the slave. The enslaved are dehumanized. The loss of social status and others' respect, personal or legal rights, dignity, and sometimes chastity characterized the slave's experience. Free men and women considered slaves to be morally inferior. Plato captures this sense of dishonor when he states: "For there is no element in the soul of a slave that is healthy."[30]

The Greek poet Homer (ca. seventh–eighth century BC), author of the *Iliad* and the *Odyssey*, describes the condition of slavery as follows:

> When the day of slavery catches up with a man, Wide-seeing Zeus takes away half of his mind.[31]

Harriet Jacobs describes this condition of dishonor, dehumanization, and degradation:

> The degradation, the wrongs, the vices, that grow out of slavery, are more than I can describe.[32]

Frederick Douglass describes how being a slave degrades a person by removing a sense of moral responsibility:

> The morality of free society can have no application to slave society.... Make a man a slave, and you rob him of moral responsibility.[33]

Shyima, the Egyptian girl who was brought to the United States and cited later in the book, offers her thoughts on this sense of inferiority inflicted on to her by her captors:

> While the entire family knew I was there to take care of anything they wanted, the Mom most of all knew how to use that power against me. She made me feel like a nobody, and I was too young and uneducated to have the skills to overcome that negative kind of thinking.

I believe that the only way I kept any dignity or sense of self was during the few hours I had to myself in the middle of the night. That was my time, and I could finally let down my guard and be me. During the day, I had to be subservient, keep my eyes lowered, and smile—even though I was often seething inside.[34]

One way for a slave to experience dishonor through a lack of identity occurs when the master gives the slave a new name and converts him or her to a new religion. Renaming the slave further depersonalizes him or her and severs any and all ties to native land, home, family, tribe, and religion:

To rob people or countries of their name is to set in motion a psychic disturbance that can, in turn, create a permanent crisis of identity.[35]

By taking away the given name and religion and assigning a new one to the slave, the master has stripped the slave of his or her old identity and furthered the power of the master in the master-slave relationship.

This practice of renaming and religious conversion may have been more challenging for the approximately 20 percent of the African exported slaves to the New World who were Muslim.[36] Those slaves who were Muslims tended to have held positions of respect within their native communities through one or more disciplines, including politics, the military, education, and their social status. Muslims had a higher probability of being literate in Arabic, the language of the Quran. They also were more resistant to change in converting to Christianity from Islam:

Muslim slaves—involuntary immigrants who had been the urban ruling elite in West Africa—constituted at least 15 percent of the slave population in North America in the eighteenth and nineteenth centuries. Their religious and ethnic roots could be traced to ancient black Islamic kingdoms in Ghana, Mali, and

Songhay. Some of these West African Muslim slaves brought the first mainstream Islamic beliefs and practices to America by keeping Islamic names, writing in Arabic, fasting during the month of Ramadan, praying five times a day, wearing modest clothing, and writing and reciting the Quran.[37]

One of the reasons that the trade in slaves was so entrenched was the need to replenish or expand the slave holdings of the community. The only slave society to increase in size due to reproduction was the United States, but the demand for slaves even exceeded the growth through reproduction. Eunuchs, whom grew in demand as Islam spread throughout northern Africa, Eurasia, Asia, and the Middle East, obviously were incapable of reproducing and there was a high mortality rate through castration. Additionally, the slave population could, and often was, reduced by manumission, particularly in the Islamic world. Other factors that fostered against a natural increase in the slave population of many societies were the high death rates due to working conditions, sacrificial rites, susceptibility to diseases in new locations, poor diets, and an imbalance of males to females. All of these dynamics created a need for replenishment that perpetuated slavery as an institution. As Paul E. Lovejoy states in *Transformations in Slavery*, "Slavery was simply not a self-sustaining institution through biological reproduction."[38]

In countries that have high poverty rates, or the areas of wealthier countries that have impoverished sections, it is not uncommon for families to sell their children to brothels. Prostitution exists in every corner of the world, and sex slavery contributes significantly to one of the world's oldest professions. The victims are beaten or threatened with violence, dehumanized, and divested of all freedom and personal rights. Their will to resist or escape has been muted. They experience natal alienation.

According to the *New York Times*, "selling naive and desperate young women into sexual bondage has become one of the fastest-growing criminal enterprises in the robust global economy."[39] As Western

Europe has become more prosperous, the demand for prostitutes has increased. Organized crime has facilitated major trafficking of women and children from Asia, the former Soviet bloc countries, and sub-Saharan Africa to Europe. The victims are lured by the false promise of jobs or marriage. Their identification papers are taken from them once they reach their destinations, and they become the property of whoever buys them. The payment for their services goes straight to the owner to repay the victim's "debt." Young girls are in particular demand because they are thought to be AIDS free. The International Organization for Migration estimates that there are 300,000 immigrant women and teenage girls in Western Europe working as prostitutes and held in debt bondage by their owners. There are widespread reports of individual experiences. The September 2003 issue of *National Geographic* relates the story of Victoria from Moldova. At age 17, she was told of a job opportunity in Turkey, but on the way, she realized that they were heading west. She was sold to a group of Serbians, who in turn sold her to a Bosnian, who then raped her along the way. Over the next several years, she was bought and sold ten times to various brothel owners. Each owner collected the money from her clients to cover her debt, which was the amount that particular brothel owner paid for her. When she resisted this treatment, she was told she would be killed. The American Anti-Slavery Group estimates that two million women and children are forced into prostitution every year as sex slaves around the globe.

Throughout history, and in modern times, slaves had skills that were highly valued by the master and his community. In many slave societies, slaves were foremen, craftsmen, carpenters, poets, musicians, solders, administrators, overseers, and household servants, in addition to being field hands and laborers. But the master always controlled the fate of the slave and the relationship was always subject to the master's caprice. The master could at any time deprive the slave of current position and relegate them to the lowest rank. Whatever was given by the master could be withdrawn.

CHAPTER TWO

Modern-Day Slavery

Differing Estimates

S LAVERY DOES NOT EXIST AS an institution officially condoned by governments in the world today. However, slavery currently exists in most areas of the world.

For myriad reasons, estimates of the extent of global slavery today vary greatly. Many countries—particularly those with the highest levels of poverty and lowest levels of literacy—still greatly underestimate levels of slavery within their borders or deny its existence entirely. There is an incentive to underplay the role of slavery in many countries as the profits for law enforcement for bribery are lucrative and sanctions from the United States are costly. The various NGOs and governmental agencies use different methodologies to estimate the number of slaves within a country. Slavery, however, is hardly a "third-world problem." The institution remains a largely intractable problem even in the world's most developed countries—including the United States.

The International Labour Organization estimates that there are 20.9 million slaves in the world, 2.2 million in state-imposed forced labor, 4.5 million in forced labor for sexual exploitation, and 14.2 million in forced labor for labor exploitation.[1]

The Walk Free Foundation's 2016 Global Slavery Index estimates that there are as many as 45.8 million people in slavery. This index ranks 167 countries based on the prevalence of slavery by population, a mea-

Global Slavery Index 2016*

(First 10 in Ranking)

Rank	Country	Est. % of Population	Est. Number of People
1	INDIA	1.4	18,354,700
2	CHINA	0.247	3,388,400
3	PAKISTAN	1.130	2,134,900
4	BANGLADESH	0.951	1,531,300
5	UZBEKISTAN	3.973	1,236,600
6	NORTH KOREA	4.373	1,100,000
7	RUSSIA	0.732	1,048,500
8	NIGERIA	0.481	875,500
9	DEMOCRATIC REPUBLIC OF CONGO	1.130	873,100
10	INDONESIA	0.286	736,100

*SOURCE: Walk Free Foundation

sure of child marriage, and trafficking in and out of the country.[2]

Free the Slaves, a human rights organization, estimates that there are between 21 and 36 million people entrapped in slavery around the world. Their estimate is that 78 percent of slavery victims are in labor slavery, while 22 percent are victims of sex slavery. They estimate that 26 percent are children. The International Labour Organization estimates that the illicit profits from slavery by traffickers are about $150 billion annually.

Slavery continues to grip the world's most developed countries. The

Percentage of Global Slavery by Region †

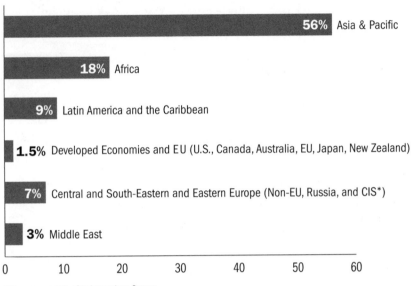

*Commonwealth of Independent States

† SOURCE: International Labor Organization

Walk Free Foundation estimates that there are 290,000 slaves in Japan; 14,500 in Germany; 6,500 in Canada; 17,500 in the Netherlands; and 11,700 in the United Kingdom.

Slavery also lives on in the United States. The US Department of State estimates that there are currently 60,000 enslaved people in the United States, compared with 57,700 in the Walk Free Foundation survey; furthermore, 15,000 to 17,500 people are trafficked into the country annually for compelled labor or commercial sex acts through the use of force, fraud, or coercion, according to the State Department.[3]

Trafficking Victims Protection Act

IN 2000, THE UNITED STATES Congress created the Trafficking Victims Protection Act (TVPA), which ranks 188 countries based on levels of slavery within their borders and their efforts to combat slavery and trafficking. The law was reauthorized in 2013. The TVPA separates sur-

27

veyed countries into three tiers. The highest grouping, Tier 1, includes all countries deemed fully compliant with the TVPA's minimum standards. The minimum standards require governments to prohibit severe forms of trafficking in persons and punishment of such acts of trafficking. The punishment should be sufficiently stringent to deter such trafficking. Among other actions, governments should vigorously investigate and prosecute trafficking, protect the victims of trafficking, cooperate with other governments in the investigation and prosecution of trafficking, monitor immigration and emigration patterns for evidence of trafficking, and track the response of law enforcement agencies to the investigation and prosecution of public officials who participate, condone, or facilitate the trafficking of persons. A Tier 1 ranking does not mean that the country has no slavery. All governments should undertake significant efforts to bring themselves into compliance with the minimum standards. The United States can consider sanctions against governments that do not comply with the minimum standards. Tier 2 countries are those that do not fully comply with the TVPA's minimum standards but are making significant efforts to do so. Finally, Tier 3 countries are those that show no effort to combat domestic slavery and are subject to international sanctions. The most important finding of the TVPA is this: of the 189 countries tracked, all are currently reported to host some level of slavery.

CHAPTER THREE

Middle East

THE MIDDLE EAST CONSISTS OF seventeen countries, an area formerly known as the Near East, centered on Western Asia and Egypt. Three major religions, Judaism, Christianity, and Islam have their origins in region. The political systems of the Middle East vary greatly from monarchies, theocracies, military dictatorships to democracies. The Islamic State (ISIS, ISIL), that controls parts of Syria and Iraq, even calls itself a caliphate.

Slavery in the Middle East has been practiced from the earliest of times. It is referenced in the written documents of the Egyptians, Sumerians, and the Code of Hammurabi of the Babylonians dating back to the eighteenth century BC. It is referenced in the Old Testament and the Talmud, as well as in the New Testament.

The Quran, Islam's holy book that dates to the seventh century AD, forms the foundation of Islam's legal and religious jurisprudence. Islam's religious law is known as Sharia Law and holds that political and religious law are inseparable. In Arabic, Sharia Law refers to God's divine law as communicated through Mohammed's preaching. Most Muslim-majority countries have contemporary legal systems that contain parts of civil, common, statutory, and religious law. For instance, many Muslim majority countries have constitutions that prohibit slavery while Sharia Law does not outlaw or prohibit slavery and slavery is practiced even though banned by statutory legislation. The Quran, Hadith (subsequent essays, reports, and rules), and Sharia Law were passed down through the generations by oral tradition and then memorialized in written Arabic texts.

Sharia Law conflicts with many Western values including representative government, human rights including women's rights, freedom of speech, private property rights, and the rule of (civil) law as well as slavery. The mix and application of different legal systems and Sharia Law is the subject of debate among Muslim scholars.

Sharia Law provides for the fair treatment of slaves and for their manumission by the master through payment or benevolence. Prisoners taken in a holy war (jihad) can be enslaved while fellow Muslims cannot be enslaved. As is often true between law (religious or civil) and practice, the instructions in the Quran regarding slavery were, and are, largely ignored.

After the death of Mohammad in AD 632, Islam spread rapidly from Arabia through Egypt and North Africa and in 711 crossed the Straits of Gibraltar onto the Iberian Peninsula. To the east and north of Mecca and Medina, Islam spread into Mesopotamia and Iran and into Central Asia and India. Islam followed the trade routes that connected North Africa to sub-Sahara Africa. Thus, Islam was initially spread by the Arab conquest of neighboring tribes to the east and west of Arabia. The conquered were slaves and, once converted to Islam, often given their freedom.

This was an enormous spread of a religion and law and brought together peoples as diverse as Middle Easterners, white Europeans, black Africans, and Asians. Many of the captives, both male and female, adopted the new religion and were absorbed into the Arab culture. Others were not. Some of the men were castrated and used as eunuchs or kept as slaves. Most of the women were used either as domestic servants or became members of the harem or concubines.

Within the Middle East today, the entirety of the Arab Gulf States that border the Persian Gulf—including Saudi Arabia, Oman, Qatar, Iraq, Kuwait, United Arab Emirates, and Bahrain—do not warrant a Tier 1 ranking by the US Department of State, meaning that they do not comply with the minimum standards of the Trafficking Victims Protection Act. Domestic workers and low-skill laborers travel between these countries looking for work and, once employed, experience forced labor, the nonpayment of wages, withholding of passports, confinement to the workplace, and long working hours without rest, all while experiencing threats or acts of violence and sexual abuse.

Other countries in the Middle East, including Tunisia, Jordan, Lebanon, Turkey, and Egypt, also do not warrant a Tier 1 ranking by the US State Department on meeting the minimum standards of the Trafficking Victims Protection Act. Iran draws a Rank of Tier 3 because the country has severe forms of human trafficking and its government is not taking significant efforts to comply with the Act. Israel and Cyprus are the only countries in the Middle East that are given a Tier 1 rank in complying with the TVPA's minimum standards on combating human trafficking.

Many Gulf States, including Saudi Arabia, Kuwait, and Qatar, are governed by a work system called "kafala." Under kafala, migrant workers must surrender their passports to the employers and cannot change or leave their job until they complete their work contract. In Saudi Arabia, this system applies even to professionals, including doctors and engineers. Employers may also withhold exit visas that are required for migrants to leave the country, thereby effectively imprisoning the worker indefinitely to forced labor. Thus, the kafala system has birthed modern-day chattel slavery, whereby the employer effectively owns the worker until their work contract, which is negotiated privately between the employer and employee, is complete. As a result, the Secretary of the International Trade Union Confederation recently described the Gulf States' labor laws as the most regressive in the world.[1]

Today, the Middle East remains a destination for impoverished immigrants and refugees from around the world—particularly Asia and Sub-Saharan Africa—who travel to the region in search of good-paying work, only to be subjected to modern-day slavery. In the Middle East and North Africa, this most often takes the form of "extortionate recruitment fees, illegal confiscation of identity documents, withholding and non-payment of salaries, hazardous working conditions, unhygienic living conditions, unlawful overtime performed under the threat of deportation, and physical and sexual abuse."[2] Forced marriage and sex trafficking, particularly of children, continues to be a widespread scourge. Finally, as the Global Slavery Index notes, the continuation and escalation of violent conflict in the Middle East and the deterioration of several economies in Sub-Saharan Africa and Asia suggest that, without significant reform, slavery in the Middle East will only increase in the coming years.[3]

EGYPT

SHYIMA EL-SAYED HASSAN WAS BORN in a small village outside of Alexandria, Egypt, one of eleven children. Shyima's father was a bricklayer and moved the family often. Despite her family's poverty, her childhood was a happy one.

When Shyima was eight years old, her sister was accused of stealing from the wealthy family for which she worked as a house servant. Knowing that Shyima's poor family could not afford to pay back the value of the stolen goods, the wealthy family convinced Shyima's family to sell Shyima to them under a contract that would last for ten years. This practice is not uncommon. In Egypt, as in other countries that experience extreme levels of poverty, parents view their children as income opportunities. The contract consigned Shyima to long hours with no days off and no pay. Shyima's only meal a day would often be after the family was finished with dinner, at which time Shyima was allowed to eat whatever scraps remained on their plates. Shyima would be physically disciplined if she misbehaved or did not complete her chores at a rate and quality satisfactory to her masters, and she never considered running away for fear of what would happen if she were captured and returned.[4]

After two years, when Shyima was ten, her masters moved to the

United States. Documents were forged so that Shyima had a passport and visa, and Shyima moved into a gated community in Irvine, California. She was consigned to a small windowless storage room in the garage that was locked at night, worked 18-hour days without a day off, and continued to survive on one meal a day and no more than a few hours of sleep. Shyima's life was one of confusion and questions left unanswered:

> These unanswered questions are typical of my life, and of the lives of many children (and adults) who are held in bondage. Slaves often lose track of family and places, and memories fade or become distorted. Unfortunately, there are thousands of us—children and adults who live their lives in slavery in Egypt, Europe, and even in the United States.[5]

Shyima had become a child slave, a debtor slave and, having been sold, a chattel slave all in one.

Two years later, a neighbor became suspicious and called Child Protective Services, who showed up at the house and rescued Shyima. Her captors were brought to trial, served three years in prison, and were forced to pay Shyima $76,137—the amount equal to the minimum wage and estimated hours Shyima had worked for the family in the United States.

Over the next several years, Shyima was placed in several foster homes, attended remedial classes in grade school, high school, and a community college. She obtained a green card, a social security number, and at the end of 2011 became a naturalized citizen of the United States. She would go on to author a book about her experiences and become a vocal anti-slavery and human rights activist.

Shyima is a modern-day slave.

Shyima is, of course, not the only documented representation of slavery in Egypt. *The Jerusalem Post* reports the experience of several survivors of kidnapping, sexual exploitation, and forced labor in the Sinai of Egypt by gangs that sought ransom for the victims.

The accounts are so shocking, the more one reads the more one becomes numb. "The kidnappers would make me lie on my back and then they would get me to ring my family to ask them to pay the ransom they wanted," 17-year-old Lamlam from Eritrea told the BBC in March last year. "As soon as one of my parents answered the phone, the men would melt flaming plastic over my back and inner thighs and I would scream and scream in pain." Another man recalled, "They had about four or five of us tied up together and they would pour water on the floor and then electrocute the water so that all of us would get electrocuted at the same time."[6]

These stories are the tip of the iceberg of a torture and mass murder industry in the Sinai Peninsula that is part of a network that spans across the Sahara and into Sudan, in which Bedouin and Somali smugglers lure Africans into camps and torture them for ransoms of up to $30,000. A survivor told Corriera Dela Serra, a human rights worker, that

> many of the women have been ferociously and repeatedly raped by Beduin who kept them in captivity in Sinai. A 33-year-old man named Temesghen told doctors, "they threatened us: 'if you don't pay we're going to take your organs.'" People were chained up for over six months; they were kept inside water tankers, in the hot and boiling sun; the women among them raped every day. And many of them were murdered.[7]

Lamlam and the others are modern-day slaves.

FrontPage Magazine, an online political magazine produced by the David Horowitz Freedom Center, a non-profit organization, published an article in November 2012 entitled "New Islamist Constitution Brings Back Slavery to Egypt." The point of the article is that the proposed constitution does not mention slavery because to them it does not exist in Egypt. This is typical of government officials who are complicit in trafficking and profiting from either commissions on trafficking revenues or through bribes and payoffs. Since slavery does not exist, there is no reason to outlaw or ban it in the new constitution. While the large caravans of the eighteenth and nineteenth centuries carrying slaves to or through Egypt have ceased, there is no question that Egypt is a source, transit, and destination for slaves. Additionally, the use of child labor, coerced or not, violates existing Egyptian laws regarding working age and minimum pay. Current Egyptian laws (outside of the Constitution) prohibit human trafficking including child marriage. These laws in Egypt, as elsewhere, have not been effective in curbing conditions of servitude.

Poverty is the cause of much of the trafficking within Egypt. Families sell their children for the money as well as to eliminate a mouth to feed. Daughters are sold to foreigners as "summer brides." Marriage brokers forge birth certificates so the girls can show that they are older. The girls are sometimes sold by the family or they are coerced or forced into the marriage. Many foreigners come to Egypt to buy child brides to take back home as domestic servants and for sexual abuse. If the child bride is sold to an Egyptian, she is forced to work or become a second wife. Many of the street children in Egypt are the product of these "summer brides" as they are abandoned by the father and the mother.

Egypt has a long history of slavery that is confirmed by a rich archeological record and writing that dates to 2,500 BC if not earlier. Archaeological evidence indicates that ancient Egyptian tribes settled along the Nile River around 4200 BC. There is evidence of social stratification, agriculture, a division of labor, and slavery around 3200 BC. Inscriptions and surviving papyrus documents all attest to the use of slaves in the household, in agriculture, and in the military throughout the history of Pharaoh Egypt, a period that stretches from about 3100 BC to 332 BC, when Alexander the Great conquered the country.

Under the Ptolemaic dynasty (ca. 332–30 BC), there are vivid reports of the harsh treatment of slaves.

In the gold mines of Nubia the slaves worked naked in dark and narrow galleries, in cramping positions, loaded with chains, and encouraged by the whip of the overseer; their food was poor, not even enough to keep them alive; thousands of them succumbed from malnutrition and fatigue; and the only welcome event in their lives was death.[8]

For the kings of Egypt gather together and condemn to the mining of the gold such as have been found guilty of some crime and captives of war, as well as those who have been accused unjustly and thrown into prison because of their anger, and not only such persons but occasionally all their relatives as well, by this means not only inflicting punishment upon those found guilty but also securing at the same time great revenues from their labours. And those who have been condemned in this way—and they are a great multitude and are all bound in chains—work at their task unceasingly both by day and throughout the entire night, enjoying no respite and being carefully cut off from any means of escape; since guards of foreign soldiers who speak a language different from theirs stand watch over them, so that not a man, either by conversation or by some contact of a friendly nature, is able to corrupt one of his keepers.... No leniency or respite of any kind is given to any man who is sick, or maimed, or aged, or in the case of a woman for her weakness, but all without exception are compelled by blows to persevere in their labours, until through ill-treatment they die in the midst of their tortures. Consequently, the poor unfortunates believe, because their punishment is so excessively severe, that the future will always be more terrible than the present and therefore look forward to death as more to be desired than life.[9]

Throughout history, war captives were often assigned to be soldiers in the military, and so it was in the Middle East and Egypt. The Arab word *mamluk* is translated to mean "slave" or "possessed." The Abbasid caliphs in Baghdad in the ninth century created a warrior class called Mamluk from captive non-Muslim slave boys. They were trained as cavalry and indoctrinated to be especially loyal to their masters and to each other. They converted to Islam during their indoctrination and training. In 1250, the Mamluk slave army of Egypt overthrew the sultan leadership of Egypt. The Mamluks eventually ruled Egypt, Syria, Nubia, and the western part of Arabia. Yet, slavery was such an accepted institution that the Mamluks continued to induct captives into their slave army. For the next 250 years, Egypt was ruled by a Mamluk sultan chosen from the Mamluk slave army.

While Egypt declared slavery illegal in 1882, slavery remains a massive and largely intractable problem in modern Egypt. According to the Walk Free Foundation's 2016 Global Slavery Index, there are an estimated 572,900 slaves currently living in Egypt. This number of slaves, which encompasses 0.626 percent of Egypt's population, is the largest in the Middle East and the eleventh largest of any country in the world. According to the US Department of State, which places Egypt as a Tier 2 government in its 2016 Trafficking in Persons Report, Egypt is both a major transit center and destination country for slaves, particularly women and children, from all over the world. The most at-risk population is the country's estimated one million street children, who are often exploited in prostitution, forced begging, and for domestic and agricultural labor, many of them immigrants and refugees from Asia, Sub-Saharan Africa, and the Middle East.[10]

The US Department of State reports that the Egyptian government does not comply with minimum standards for the elimination of trafficking but observes that it is making significant progress. For instance, the country "continues to lack formal victim identification procedures and protection services, and some victims of trafficking are punished for acts committed as a direct result of being trafficked." However, the government has taken some steps to combat domestic servitude and child sex tourism and to raise awareness of the trafficking problem within Egypt.[11]

QATAR

VICTORIA ARRIVED IN QATAR FROM the Philippines to work as a domestic assistant for a wealthy family in Doha. Initially, she worked eighteen-hour days, but for a monthly salary at a living wage and regular days off.

However, as time passed, her workload increased dramatically. Visiting family members arrived, and for two months Victoria served them around the clock with no days off. Finally, Victoria asked her employers to pay her to reflect the additional time she had worked. In response, they docked her wages, gave her no days off, and cut her off from all communication with her friends and family.[12]

Like Victoria, Angelica was brought to Qatar from the Philippines and promised work as a domestic worker for a wealthy family. After several months, Angelica responded to a summons from her employer; according to Angelica, he smelled like alcohol and became aggressive. When Angelica tried to escape, she fell violently, breaking both of her legs and feet and fracturing her spine. As she lay on the ground, unable to move, begging him not to harm her, he proceeded to sexually assault her.[13]

Victoria and Angelica are modern-day slaves.

Qatar is located on the eastern border of Saudi Arabia in the Persian Gulf. It was formerly part of the Ottoman Empire and after WWI became a British protectorate, gaining independence in 1971. It is an absolute monarchy with a constitution, adopted in 2003, that is based largely on Islam's Sharia Law, with touches of civil law.

In terms of total land area, the Gulf state of Qatar is the 164th largest country in the world. Its 11,500 square miles make it the same size as the little-known territory of Nagorno Karabakh and only 595 square miles larger than the tropical island of Jamaica.

Qatar's relevance in world economics and politics, however, greatly overshadows its meager territory. Once a poor British protectorate for whom pearls were the most significant export, Qatar ranks as one of the richest countries in the world as measured on a GDP per capita basis. A single force has transformed Qatar: the oil and gas industry.[14] Despite its small size, Qatar sits on the world's 14th largest reserve of oil. Black gold does not just form the country's backbone: earnings from the hydrocarbon sector accounted for 60 percent of the country's total government revenues and 58 percent of its total GDP over the past five years.[15]

Qatar's oil boom created an economic vacuum and a resulting demand for labor that the country's tiny population could not possibly support. According to findings from an International Trade Union Confederation investigation, roughly 88 percent of Qatar's population is made up of migrant workers, predominantly from Bangladesh, India, Pakistan, the Philippines, and Sri Lanka.[16] According to the report, most stories are similar: poor workers from other Gulf states "came to Qatar with optimism and good will, only to face despair when their employer decides they are disposable and refuses to pay wages, sacks them without benefits and/or refuses to sign their exit permit." Massive labor camps, in which hundreds of thousands of workers and children live in abject poverty and constant squalor, paint a vivid picture of the country's rampant inequality and slave reality.[17]

With an estimated 30,300 slaves in a total population of 2.235 million, Qatar has the fifth highest prevalence of slavery in the world and the highest in either the Middle East or North Africa. In the 2016 Global Slavery Index, Qatar is ranked in the world's bottom dozen in government response to their slavery epidemic. The Walk Free Foundation calls Qatar "a destination for the exploitation of men and women from Asia who travel to the Gulf nation with promises of well-paid jobs." The country's kafala sponsorship system "effectively ties a migrant worker's legal status to the employer," as "workers are unable to leave the country or seek alternative employment without their sponsor's written consent." Any attempt by an exploited worker to escape can result in jail time for "absconding." Qatar's National Human Rights Committee states that domestic workers are particularly at risk, as "they are most exposed to transgressions, due to the lack of legislation to regulate their affairs and employment relationships, and the fact that they are not subject" to the country's baseline labor laws.[18]

SAUDI ARABIA

LOCATED ON THE ARABIAN PENINSULA, The Kingdom of Saudi Arabia was founded in 1932 by Ibn Saud after he conquered and united several tribes within the region. The political system is a hereditary monarchy based on Islam's Sharia Law. According to Human Rights Watch and Amnesty International, the government is considered one of the most repressive regimes in the world in terms of human rights. There are no political parties, no elections, and no religious freedoms. It is an absolute monarchy.

As for many of its neighbors in the Middle East, oil is the lifeblood of Saudi Arabia's economy. Saudi Arabia is the world's largest oil exporter, and oil accounts for roughly 80 percent of budget revenues and 45 percent of GDP. According to the World Bank, Saudi Arabia's GDP—$646 billion in 2015—is the 20th largest in the world, and its GDP per capita ranks in the top 10.

Saudi Arabia's economic success stands in striking contrast to its response to modern-day slavery. The 2016 Global Slavery Index notes that Saudi Arabia's slavery problem, with slaves numbering 92,100, is particularly striking because, like Kuwait and Hong Kong, Saudi Arabia is one of the most developed economies to exhibit such a poor response to modern slavery.[19]

Anecdotal evidence also highlights the wide acceptance of slavery within the country: in 2012, a man was discovered trying to sell a castrated male slave on Facebook.[20] Also in 2012, a Saudi prince was found guilty of sexually abusing and murdering a slave that he had brought with him from Saudi Arabia to London.[21]

The International Labour Organization estimates that Saudi Arabia has among the highest number of foreign domestic help workers in the world. Like Qatar, Saudi Arabia imports nearly 90 percent of its workers, most of them from neighboring Gulf states and Nepal, Pakistan, India, and Bangladesh. As in all countries, domestic help workers are particularly vulnerable to exploitation because of the isolation of working in private homes. As in other Arab countries, the kafala system requires "sponsoring" employers to give written consent for workers to change jobs.[22]

The US State Department places Saudi Arabia as a Tier 2 Watch List country, meaning that it is vulnerable to being downgraded to a Tier 3 status.

YEMEN

YEMEN IS AN ARAB COUNTRY located on the southwestern end of the Arabian Peninsula. It has a history of instability as competing religious, tribal, regional, political, and foreign powers have jockeyed for control over time. Yemen is currently in the grips of a civil war, with Iran and Saudi Arabia backing opposing forces. For this reason, reliable figures are difficult to come by, but the United Nations reports that human rights violations are rampant.[23]

According to the 2016 Global Slavery Index, there are an estimated 303,200 slaves currently living in Yemen, equating to 1.13 percent of the population. According to a recent report by Anti-Slavery International, Yemen is a country of transit and destination for trafficked adults from Southern and East Africa, many of them on their way to Saudi Arabia.

Yemen currently lacks any substantive legislation regarding trafficking in persons. Domestic workers are not legally recognized as workers and lack any protections under the country's labor code.[24]

The US Department of State designated Yemen as a special case because of the difficulty of obtaining information due to the civil war.

41

The report does note that vulnerable populations in Yemen were at increased risk of human trafficking due to large-scale violence driven by ongoing armed conflict, civil unrest, and lawlessness. The report also notes the increase in the recruitment and use of children as young as ten throughout the country by government forces and militias as soldiers. Prior to the escalation of armed conflict in 2015, the report estimated that there were as many as 1.7 million children laborers under the age of 14 in Yemen. That would represent an astonishing 6.3 percent of the population.

TURKEY

TWO MEN APPROACHED AN IMPOVERISHED young Russian woman and promised her a well-paying job in Istanbul. When she arrived in Turkey to meet her employer, she was violently kidnapped. Her passport and money were confiscated, and she was taken to a brothel and forced into prostitution. The brothel owner charged her the sum he had paid to purchase her and an exorbitant amount for room and board—enough that she could never hope to pay off her debts.

Eventually, while with a customer, the young woman attempted to jump to her freedom through an unlocked window. The customer alerted the brothel owner, who retrieved her broken body from the street. Instead of taking her to the hospital, he returned her to the brothel, where she would die.[25] This young woman is a modern-day slave. The story is typical of how perpetrators recruit victims of slavery throughout the world.

The Republic of Turkey is located on the Anatolian Peninsula between Europe and Asia. In 1299, a confederation of Turkic tribes founded the Ottoman Empire just south of Constantinople, which over time became an Islamic transcontinental caliphate that controlled large portions of Western Asia, Southeast Europe, the Middle East, North Africa, and Eastern Africa. The Empire reached its peak in the sixteenth century, then began a long decline, culminating with its defeat at the end of WWI in 1919. After a three-year war of independence (1919–1922), Turkey became a sovereign nation in 1923. The march towards a multi-party democracy has been interrupted by several military interventions by the Turkish armed forces. A failed coup by the military occurred in the summer of 2016. Today, Turkey is a parliamentary democracy with a secular constitution. The majority of the people are Muslim.

During the expansion of the Ottoman Empire in Eurasia from the thirtieth century to the sixteenth century, captives in war were kept as slaves by the conquers or were sold. Indeed, the revenues from the sale of slaves were an important part of the economy, as slaves were used in all aspects of daily life as well as in the military. When there were periods of peace between the Ottomans and the surrounding political entities, the Ottomans would engage in raiding their neighbors for slaves to sell on the various slave markets. Whether during times of peace or expansion, the capture of soldiers as slaves or the raiding and kidnapping of foreigners as slaves was justified under Islamic law since the majority of these people were infidels. There are reports of expeditions that resulted in the mass enslavement of as many as 50,000 captives.

> In the period extending from about 1260–1390, the age of the great expansion of the Anatolian Turks into Byzantine territories in western Anatolia and Thrace and into Macedonia and Bulgaria, captives flowed into the Ottoman lands in great numbers. It can even be added that during this period the great demand for slaves from the Islamic hinterland and the rising prices played an important part in the extension of the raids and consequently the rise of the prosperous principalities in Western Anatolia. Paradoxically enough not only for the slave markets in Italy but also for agricultural labor in their Levantine colonies, Venetians and Genoese too became regular customers of these principalities....

It should be noted that particular ethnic groups among the slaves in the Ottoman empire or among those purchased by foreigners became dominant at given periods of time depending on where Ottoman raiding was then intense. In the fourteenth century, Greeks and Bulgarians, in the fifteenth century, Serbs, Albanians, Wallachians, Bosnians; and in the sixteenth century, Hungarians, Italians, Germans, Italians, Spaniards and Georgians....

Sahib Giray Khan (1532–1551) [a leader under the Ottoman Sultan]... was also responsible for large scale expeditions into Circassia which resulted in mass enslavements. In the 1530s Kansavuk, Circassian chieftain of the Jana agreed to send a yearly tribute of one thousand slaves to the Ottoman Sultan and five hundred to the Khan. Upon his failure to keep his promise, Sahib Giray led an expedition against him in 1539, and took, according to his court chronicler, 50,000 captives.[26]

The establishment of Russian dominance in Eastern Europe and the Russian annexation of the Crimea in 1783 finally ended the profitable trade of the Tatars and Ottomans, who for centuries had reaped an annual harvest of slaves from the villages of the Ukraine and adjoining lands and exported their crop to the slave markets of Istanbul, Cairo, and other Ottoman cities. The once-plentiful supply of white slaves from Central and Western Europe had long since dwindled to a mere trickle, and after the Russian annexation of the Caucasian lands circa 1801–1828, the last remaining source of white slaves for the Islamic world was reduced and finally stopped.[27]

Female slaves from the Caucasian area were highly prized in Turkey and Egypt and brought a high price. They were used as household help and as concubines and in harems. "As the supply of white slaves from Circassia and Georgia sharply declined, the Egyptian market turned increasingly to the abundant source of black slaves from the region of the Upper Nile."[28]

The 2016 Global Slavery Index estimates that there are 480,300 living in slavery today in Turkey, amounting to 0.626 percent of the country's total population, "reflecting high numbers of child marriage, forced labor, and trafficking for sexual exploitation." The Global Slavery Index also rates Turkey as the most vulnerable state in Eurasia due to its high levels of irregular migration, proximity to conflict zones in Syria and Iraq, and high levels of discrimination against the country's minority groups. Turkey is experiencing the largest influx of refugees from the civil war in Syria of any country in the Middle East or Europe. These refugees are at risk of slavery due to their impoverished and desperate situation.

There are numerous reports of The Islamic State of Iraq (ISIS), also called The Islamic State of the Levant (ISIL), enslaving their captives in Syria and Iraq and either keeping them or selling them into Turkey. The following paragraphs are from a release by the Gatestone Institute entitled "ISIS Selling Yazidi Women and Children in Turkey," dated December 20, 2015. The article was written by Uzay Bulut, a Turkish journalist based in Ankara.

> The latest reports reveal that in Turkey, a country that fancies itself as a candidate for EU membership, Yazidi women and children are enslaved and forced into sexual slavery. Meanwhile, the Turkish government has not bothered to make a single statement about these reports.
>
> IS [Islamic State] offers women and underage children in a kind of virtual slave market with for-sale photos.... The transfer of money, as the reporter discovered, takes place through a liaison office in Turkey.
>
> Five thousand people have been taken as captives. Women and children are raped, and then sold. These must be considered crimes.
>
> An office has been established by ISIS members in Antep

[Turkey]; and at that office, women and children kidnapped by ISIS are sold for high amounts of money. Where are the ministers and law enforcement officials of this country who are talking about stability?[29]

In June of 2016, the Parliamentary Assembly of the Council of Europe stated that "recent developments in Turkey pertaining to freedom of the media and of expression, erosion of the rule of law and the human rights violations in relation to anti-terrorism security operations in south-east Turkey have … raised serious questions about the functioning of its democratic institutions."[30]

Necla Kelek was born in Turkey, emigrated to Germany, and earned a PhD in Islamic Studies. She has written extensively on the exposure of Turkish-born women to arranged and forced marriage to German Turkish men. She contends that tens of thousands of Turkish women have been sold to German-Turkish men as brides and are held in slave-like conditions once the marriage has been consummated. She equates these forced marriages to modern-day slavery.

Ms. Kelek's great-grandfather was a slave trader. He kidnapped or purchased beautiful white Caucasian women from the Caucasian area of central Asia and sold them to sultans. This followed a tradition whereby between 1530 and 1780 some 1.2 million white Christian women from the Caucasus were sold to the slave markets in North Africa, according to her research.[31]

The United States Department of State states that Turkey is a source, destination, and transit country for women, men, and children subjected to sex trafficking and forced labor. Foreign victims are offered cleaning and childcare jobs in Turkey and upon arrival, traffickers confiscate their passports and force them into prostitution in hotels, discos, and homes. Turkish women are subject to sex trafficking within the country and Western Europe. Traffickers increasingly use psychological coercion, threats, and debt bondage to compel victims into sex trafficking. The

State Department's Tier 2 ranking means that the Government of Turkey does not fully comply with the minimum standards for the elimination of trafficking.

UNITED ARAB EMIRATES

THE UNITED ARAB EMIRATES (UAE) is one of the richest countries in the world. Awash in oil wealth and touting a highly developed finance sector, the UAE's moderate foreign policy stance has made the UAE a vital player in world affairs, despite its small size and population.[32] According to the 2016 Global Slavery Index, an estimated 37,000 slaves live in the United Arab Emirates out of a population of 9.1 million (0.4 percent of the population), ranking the country third in the Middle East.[33]

According to the country's 2010 census, the UAE's population is 88 percent foreign and only 12 percent nationals. The United States Department of State estimates that migrant workers comprise over 95 percent of the country's private sector workforce. The Global Slavery Index calls the UAE's government response to modern slavery the most comprehensive in the Middle East. However, the country still lags behind many countries in other regions. For instance, while prostitution is illegal in the UAE, women and young children brought to the country for employment as domestic workers and waitresses often find themselves forced to provide sexual services to pay back their travel and visa costs, often in an unending spiral of debt bondage. Further, the country's massive population of migrant domestic workers remain at risk, particularly under the country's strong kafala sponsorship program. These workers are often held hostage through nonpayment of wages, physical abuse, restrictions on movement and travel, and the unlawful withholding of passports.

The US Department of State wrote in its most recent Trafficking in Persons Report that while the Government of the United Arab Emirates does not fully comply with the minimum standards for the elimination of trafficking, it is making significant efforts to do so. For instance, the government has made "sustained, but uneven, progress" in providing protective services to trafficking victims, though the number of prosecutions and convictions of trafficking offenders has decreased in recent years. It is given a Tier Ranking of 2.[34]

SYRIA

SYRIA IS LOCATED IN WESTERN ASIA, surrounded by the Mediterranean Sea, Turkey, Iraq, Jordan, and Israel. Formerly part of the Ottoman Empire, it became a French mandate after WW I and gained its independence in 1945. Since independence the country has experienced political instability, a number of military dictatorships, and since 1970, ruled by the Assad family as a non-democratic Islamic state.

Since the beginning of the protests against the Assad regime in 2011, more than 400,000 people have been killed and another nine million have been displaced in Syria's civil war. In fact, Syria's refugee population is currently the largest in the world and the second largest in recorded history. This humanitarian crisis has created a flood of at-risk Syrian refugees into the modern slavery pipelines of other countries in the Middle East and made Syria a key source and destination for forced labor and sex trafficking victims.[35]

Violent conflict and political instability has contributed to Syria becoming one of the countries with the weakest responses to the slavery epidemic: in the 2016 Global Slavery Index, Syria has the sixth highest proportion of its population in slavery—257,300 out of a population of 22.8 million (1.13 percent). An estimated 80 percent of school-aged Syrian children work, many in the fields and as street vendors. Government instability has allowed a number of armed, non-state militant groups, including the Free Syrian Army, the Kurdish People Protection Units, and the Islamic State to purchase the children of impoverished or displaced families.

Forced and child marriage are also growing problems. In 2011, 13 percent of Syrian girls under 18 were married, and that number rose to

25 percent in 2013. In 2016, the US Department of State determined that the Syrian government does not comply with the minimum standards for the elimination of trafficking and is not making significant efforts to do so and rank it a Tier 3 country.

Women move bricks. In India women balance stacks of bricks on their heads to carry them to nearby trucks. Each brick weighs about six pounds.
PHOTOGRAPH BY LISA KRISTINE.

Children work in unbearable heat. Forced child labor in a brick kiln factory in Nepal.
PHOTOGRAPH BY LISA KRISTINE.

In Nepal, kiln workers stacking bricks on their heads to carry to their destination.
PHOTOGRAPH BY LISA KRISTINE.

Brothers carrying stone in the Himalayas. Each day, children make several trips down the mountain with very heavy loads.
PHOTOGRAPH BY LISA KRISTINE.

Gold in poisoned water. Slaves pan for gold, wading in water poisoned by mercury used in the extraction process.
PHOTOGRAPH BY LISA KRISTINE.

A family portrait in toxic color: blue, red, black. Photograph taken at a textile factory in India, where families are enslaved in the production and dyeing of silk using toxic dyes.
PHOTOGRAPH BY LISA KRISTINE.

Migrant workers on their way to a construction site, in Phuket Town, Thailand, October 13, 2013.
PHOTOGRAPH BY 1000 WORDS/SHUTTERSTOCK.COM.

Sulfur miners extracting sulfur inside the crater of Kaweh Ijen Volcano in East Java, Indonesia. Very dangerous work in toxic sulfur fumes and fog.
PHOTOGRAPH BY R. M. NUNES/SHUTTERSTOCK.COM.

For additional information about these photographs, please see "Image and Photographic Credits" section on pages 211–212.

CHAPTER FOUR

Africa

"OUR DAY BEGAN AT 5 AM. Carrying heavy tools on our heads, we had to walk six kilometres through mud and stones in bare feet to reach the fields. By the time we reached them we were soaked through and exhausted. Once we arrived the overseer showed us the area we each had to plant before the day's end. We were afraid of what he would do to us if we could not finish the work. This threat and the threat of being denied food if we could not finish in time forced us to work quickly. The work was hard and bending all day gave us back pains. If we were ill and couldn't work, we were afraid that we would be tortured to death. One day I witnessed two of my colleagues being tortured for trying to escape. They became seriously ill and died."[1]

This was the tale of a young boy trafficked to a cocoa farm in the Ivory Coast. He is a modern-day slave.

Africa has a long history of Africans enslaving Africans. The early Arab and European explorers encountered a thriving slave trade among Africans. The sources of slaves were the same as in almost all societies that practiced slavery: captives in war, kidnapped persons, and debtor slaves. An Arab observer in the Ghana Empire wrote in the twelfth century his observation of the slave trade:

> The people of Barisa, Silla, and Ghana raid the country of the Lamlam, capture its inhabitants, and bring them to their own countries, where they sell them to merchants who come there. The latter export them to other countries.[2]

This flourishing trade was ongoing four centuries before Columbus sailed to the New World.

Sub-Saharan Africa is generally considered to be the geographic area that lies south of the Sahara Desert. The Sahel is the area between the Sahara Desert and the savanna that lies to the south. To the north of the Sahara Desert lie the countries that border the Mediterranean Sea. Several countries in Africa border the transition areas of these geographic zones. This report will cover some but not all the countries within Africa and generally classify them as Central, Southern, Southeastern, and Western Africa.

The Sahara began to dry up around 3000 BC, with the area reaching full desiccation around 1500 BC. As the Sahara turned to sand, the Arabs, Berbers, and Moors migrated south from North Africa and mixed with the sub-Saharan black Africans.

African life during the ancient and medieval period was based upon kinship. The political organizations of Africa varied widely but formed based on the simplest political formation: the family. The larger the family size, the larger the political, and perhaps military power of the kinship group. Slavery would increase the size of the kinship group without the constraint of genetics. Thus, slaves were allowed to assimilate into the kinship group, but the master retained arbitrary control over the fate of the slave. The impact of assimilation created a constant need for new slaves. As water flows into and then out of a sink, an assimilated slave needed to be replaced. This need for replenishment sustained the institution of slavery. Thus, the instruments of acquisition: wars, raids, kidnapping, or purchasing, were ongoing. Once slavery became the principal means of production in agriculture after the introduction of New World crops, slavery could only be sustained by replenishment, since kinship groups did not reproduce sufficiently to add to their size, and mortality rates exceeded birth rates.

Generally, several families would form a clan or tribe, and to protect from outside threats or through the emergence of a strong leader, a group of tribes would eventually form a village and city-state, and then a kingdom or empire. In the more arid regions, nomadic tribes would follow wild game for food or the rains with their herds of goats and cattle.

The tribes of West Africa and the tribes of North Africa along the Mediterranean coast established trade routes through the Sahara, and the spread of Islam along the caravan trade routes in the seventh and eight centuries introduced literacy, along with science, bureaucracy, and the codification of laws and justice. The trans-Saharan trade routes allowed the Arab and Berber Muslim traders to penetrate West Africa as far south as modern-day Ghana, Nigeria, and the Ivory Coast. Over time, the caste system developed whereby the northern Berbers and Moors came to dominate the Africans. To the east, the Nile River was an important trade route that linked the eastern Mediterranean countries to central and eastern Africa as far back as the historical record can be traced.

The inhabitants of modern Africa vary greatly in race, and in ethnic and tribal groups. However, the ancestors of all were victims of, or participated in, the ancient slave trade and practiced slavery. Although the colonial European powers abolished the slave trade and slavery in their African possessions in the nineteenth century, the laws were not enforced and the practice continued even as the former colonies gained their independence. Slavery exists today in every country in Africa even though all have outlawed the legal practice of slavery, thus confirming the theme of this book: the legal prohibition against slavery has not ended its practice.

CENTRAL AFRICA

SEVERAL SUB-SAHARA AFRICAN COUNTRIES in central Africa have received the US State Department's lowest ranking in 2016—Tier 3—for inability and lack of effort to control and curb modern-day slavery. These countries include the Sudan, South Sudan, The Central African Republic, Burundi, Eritrea, and Zimbabwe. The Democratic Republic of the Congo, Republic of Congo, and Rwanda are on a Tier 2 Watch List. Selected countries will be covered as follows.

SUDAN AND SOUTH SUDAN

Mende Nazer lived in a remote village in the Nuba Mountains in southern Sudan as a member of the Karko tribe. She was twelve years old and a Muslim. While her village was rural and the huts made of mud brick with thatched straw roofs, her family was considered middle class. Her father owned a herd of fifty cattle and she attended school, aspiring to be a doctor. In school, she studied Arabic and the beginnings of English. The fields around the village were planted in sorghum, the staple crop, and the livestock consisted of cattle, some goats, and chickens. The men also hunted the countryside for animals to supplement the homegrown diet.

One night she awoke to the sound of horse hoofs, gunfire, screaming, a vision of fire, and the smell of smoke. Her village had become engulfed in a commotion and chaos of unimaginable proportions. Her father yelled, "Arab raiders! The Mujahedin are in the village!"

The raiders killed the men, raped and killed the women, and captured the children, both girls and boys. Before dragging the younger women off as captives, they pinned them to the ground, ripped their clothes off and raped them, some as young as nine or ten. They slit the throats of the babies and the pregnant women. They torched all the huts, and left the village a smoldering debris of ashes. The Mujahedin are Arab militia. They are also slave traders.

The raiders took the captives on horseback to a Sudanese government army camp, near the town of Dilling and sold them to a slave dealer. From there, the children were loaded into trucks destined for Khartoum. Once Mende was in Khartoum, she was sold to a family as a domestic slave, and her master kept her in a small brick shed in an alleyway at the side of the house. After performing her daily duties, which took up to sixteen hours a day, she was locked in the shed at night. If she displeased her master she was beaten. She was never paid. Mende describes her feelings as follows:

> I was overcome with grief. But, more than anything, I was filled with an intense loneliness. I had been enfolded with love and kindness all my life. Now I was completely and utterly alone.[3]

It took Mende a while to realize what had happened to her. She knew some Arabic from school but not enough to understand a full sentence. However, she did pick up the Arabic word for slave, *abda* (*abeed* for plural), when she was passed from one slave trader to the next:

> I suddenly remembered the story my father told me about the Arabs who had raided the Shimii village. He said they had taken the girls as "abeed"—as slaves. Now I finally knew what Rahab was calling me. She was calling me her slave. [4]

Mende worked for her master for close to seven years, all the while receiving no compensation. She never left the house unescorted. After years as a domestic slave with the family in Khartoum, Mende was sold or given to her master's sister in London, a place she had never heard of. Before she left for London, Mende met her replacement, a Nuba girl named Nanu. Her story was similar to Mende's. Arab raiders sacked her village, killing, raping, and capturing the children. The raiders raped Nanu as they took her and the other captive children to the Sudanese government army camp. The raiders sold the children to a slave dealer who, in turn, sold the children to families in Khartoum as domestic slaves.

Mende's master in London turned out to be a Sudanese Arab working for the Sudanese Embassy. At the time, he was the Acting Ambassador. Her life in London was no better than in Khartoum. She was confined to the house and worked sixteen-hour days. She had no days off and received no pay. At one point, she even contemplated suicide.

Mende decided that she had to escape, and the plan to do so was aided by her master's vacation to Sudan. She was assigned to live with a family friend of her master. They treated her well and she contacted a free person from the Sudan. Upon return of the master from the Sudan, she ran away and sought asylum in England. During the two years it took to gain asylum, Mende, along with Damien Lewis, wrote the book *Slave: My True Story*, which became a best seller.[5]

Mende is a modern-day slave.

Abuk Bak is from Achuru, a village in southern Sudan, and was captured by Arab militia. She was twelve years old at the time. As was true in the previous case, the militia set fire to the houses with their thatched, grass roofs, shot the men, and captured the women and children. They also took the livestock as part of their plunder. Abuk Bak and the others were taken to a town called Daien and herded into a fenced pen. All along the Arab militia kept calling the captives *abeeda*, a variation of *abeed*, the Arab word for "slaves." The next day the pen turned out to be a slave market and the captives were sold to the highest bidders:

> The turbaned men observed us and pointed at different people, choosing which person they wanted to buy, the same way they chose their goats and cows from the pens around us. They didn't bother to look us over to see if we were healthy or strong; if we got sick or died they could just buy someone else to do their work. I watched them as they yelled and pointed until finally they settled on a deal. Then one of the Arabs from the raid would charge in between us and drag one of us out to her new master. I heard the word again, *Abeeda, Abeeda*. They also watched us to make sure we didn't make any trouble or try to escape. If anyone did, they would be beaten or killed. [6]

Abuk was sold to a cattle and goat herder who lived with his wife and two children in a tent-like dwelling made of cow hide. She spent the next ten years doing housework for the wife and tending the livestock for the husband. She was often beaten, fed a subsistence amount of food, frequently consisting of left-over scraps. She was never paid.

> The loneliness of my life with Ahmed Adam and his family was overwhelming. I would go days, even weeks at a time without speaking to anyone. It took me years to understand any part of the few words they said to me. Even the word *abeeda* was still a mystery to me with no one there to explain its meaning. After I refused to learn to pray with the Koran, Ahmed Adam stopped trying to teach me anything, and my days were filled with silence.[7]

Abuk eventually escaped and received refugee status from the United Nations. She now lives with her three children in the United States, where she frequently lectures about the existence of slavery in the Sudan.

Abuk is a modern-day slave.

Francis Bok, an associate at the American Anti-Slavery Group, wrote a book entitled *Escape from Slavery: The True Story of My Ten Years in Captivity and My Journey to Freedom in America*. Bok was taken captive at the age of seven during an Arab raid of his village in southern Sudan. He was sold into slavery and endured daily beatings and the mental and physical humiliation and degradation of chattel slavery. He finally escaped, only to be imprisoned in Khartoum. Upon his release, he fled to Egypt and sought asylum through the United Nations, which relocated him to the United States.

Bok is a modern-day slave.

Simon Deng is a Sudanese Christian who was kidnapped into slavery at the age of nine by the northern Arab militia. It was a frequent and condoned event for the Muslim Arab north, who ruled the country, to raid, kidnap, and enslave southern Muslim and Christian blacks. After Simon was captured he was held as a slave for three years in conditions similar to those of other Sudanese described in the earlier part of this narrative. He was beaten, given scraps to eat, and threatened with violence if he tried to escape. He eventually did flee and became something of a national hero by becoming a swimming champion. He describes the situation in Sudan and Southern Sudan:

> According to the Sudanese government, the African culture is a savage culture that needs to be changed and transformed into the Arab culture. Three point five million were killed in southern Sudan in the name of Islam between 1955 and 2005, seven million southern Sudanese Christians became refugees, and a quarter million Nubians were slaughtered.

> They're killing these people because they made a big mistake: they took Islamization, but they didn't take Arabization. They didn't take the whole package, and they are paying a price today.[8]

In June 2015, Deng engaged in a hunger strike to bring attention to the continued fighting and loss of life in the southern Sudan. He was appealing to President Obama to intervene. To date, the United States has sent only humanitarian relief to the area.

Deng is a modern-day slave.

Mende, Bok, Abuk and Deng are but four of the thousands of southern and eastern (Darfur) Sudanese who have been kidnapped or captured by Arab militia and sold into slavery. Virtually every week there are reports in the national newspapers of Arab militia raids on the villages of Southern Sudan and Darfur. The conflict in Southern Sudan has left nearly three million people homeless and forced one million to flee.[9]

In the 2016 Global Slavery Index, Sudan ranks 6th in percentage of population living in slavery, with an estimated 454,700 slaves (1.13 percent of the total population) currently living within its territory. Meanwhile, an estimated 139,400 slaves (1.13 percent of the total population of 12.3 million) currently live in South Sudan.[10]

The 2014 Global Slavery Index observes that "there are very few countries with a history so intrinsically linked to slavery as Sudan." While modern-day slavery in Sudan and Southern Sudan takes many forms, the 2014 Index cites domestic work, commercial exploitation, and forced child marriages as the most prevalent and problematic. Particularly concerning is the trafficking of refugees from Eritrea who are often bought by Sudanese traffickers and sold to Egyptian traders for export around the world. Further, lack of safety and economic opportunity in Sudan forces many citizens to seek employment in surrounding countries, and "a complex web of brokers and recruitment agencies operate to deceive Sudanese nationals" by promising jobs and transportation but instead selling these would-be immigrants into forced labor.[11] Furthermore, child prostitution and exploitation of child laborers in agriculture and other sectors continues to rise in both Sudan and South Sudan.[12]

The Government of Sudan enacted a new anti-trafficking law, increased the legal minimum age of military recruitment to 18 years, rescued and aided a growing number of slaves, and made increased efforts to detect and capture traffickers. The picture painted of South Sudan's response, however, is less promising: the State Department's report states that the Government of South Sudan did not investigate or prosecute a single trafficking offense, that law enforcement presence and capacity in most of the country lacked any ability to curb trafficking, and that the government and police continued to arrest and jail women and girls in the slave trade—many of whom claimed to be victims of trafficking—instead of their traffickers.

One might wonder why the millions of other slaves in the world today and in the past did not take steps to escape or otherwise free themselves. Indeed, throughout history some slaves did attempt to seek freedom as history is replete with slave revolts, fugitive slaves, runaways, and slaves buying their freedom. Mende did escape eventually. However, Mende and the others who escaped are the exceptions. Many obstacles stand between slaves and freedom.

Mende's tribal language was not known to most of the peoples in Khartoum or London. She had never been to a large city before, and cities can be quite intimidating for a young village girl. She was physically constrained. She was dehumanized. As Mende states:

> "I had spent three long years completely under Rahab's con-
> trol. She had beaten me, abused me, and killed any sense I
> once had of my own worth. I believed that I was her slave and
> that she was my master. I believed that she was in absolute
> control and that she held the power of life or death over me.[13]
> After all those years, Rahab had completely destroyed my
> sense of my own identity and my own self-worth. I believed
> that I was no longer valuable as a human being."[14]

The will of the slave is broken. The master reduces the status of the
slave to a sub-human. Through the threat of violence, the isolation,
the master's power to control the life or death of the enslaved, the
humiliation, the lack of self-worth, the master reduces the slave to a
condition of total obedience and obsequiousness. The slave has been
trained to submit and consequently has no will to resist or escape. Similar attitudes have been expressed by the survivors of the Nazi death
camps. One loses the will to live. This mental condition is difficult for
free people to grasp.

Mende, as well as the others cited above, was a slave under the accepted definition of slavery. She was captured or kidnapped in a raid
on her village. She was sold by the raiders to a slave trader. The slave
trader sold her to a master. She was chattel property. She was divested of all freedom and personal rights. She was owned by and totally
subject to the will of her master, who could sell, loan, gift, bequest,
or otherwise dispose of her. She experienced natal alienation (family separation), violence, and dishonor. She was dehumanized by her
master through psychological and physical means practiced over long
periods of time. The conditions surrounding her slave-master relationship drained away all power to resist. She lost her identity and sense of
kinship with humanity.

60

DEMOCRATIC REPUBLIC OF THE CONGO and THE CENTRAL AFRICAN REPUBLIC

> I have trouble believing that such a level of horror is possible. Victims have been held as sex slaves—sometimes for months at a time. Militia members simply show up, steal what they can, and take men and women out of local communities who are then kept captive under the most horrendous conditions for months at a time.[15]

This was the report of a worker for the humanitarian group Médecins Sans Frontières in the gold and diamond regions in eastern Democratic Republic of the Congo.

Widespread violence caused by ethnic, tribal, and civil war has plagued the Democratic Republic of the Congo (DRC) and the Central African Republic (CAR) for decades. These armed conflicts have been fueled and funded by the profits from the extraction of minerals worth billions of dollars to the outside world. The sale of these natural resources, including diamonds, gold, timber, tantalum, coltan (columbite-tantalite), and cassiterite provide the funds for the warlords, rebels, vigilantes, and other armed groups to buy arms and munitions. Coltan is used in the production of capacitors and is only found in the Congo and Tanzania. These natural resources are often called conflict minerals or blood diamonds. They are called such because they are produced by slave labor.[16]

The Democratic Republic of the Congo (DRC), formerly the Belgian Congo and Zaire, is technically a semi-presidential republic, gaining its independence in 1960. Since then, it has experienced political and social instability. The CAR, a former French colony, also gained independence in 1960 and has experienced similar instability.

Research by several human rights non-profits as well as governmental reports including the United States Department of State confirm that forced labor, peonage, child slavery, sexual slavery, debt bondage, and child soldiers are widespread. Child slavery is particularly prominent in that children are easily coerced, illiterate, respond to violence or the threat of violence, and will work just to be fed. Reports also estimate that upwards of 90 percent of men working in the mines are victims of debt bondage. The employers charge the workers for the tools they use, the food they eat, and accommodations plus interest. The pay the workers receive is purposely set below the repayment schedules, so the workers are perpetual debt slaves. They are forced to continue working to pay off constantly accumulating debt that is passed from one generation to the next: descent-based slavery.

The armed groups raid villages and kidnap and capture women and children who are forced to work in the mines. The women and girls are forced into sexual slavery at night after working in the mines during the day. Children are particularly sought after because they can crawl into areas of the mines that an adult body cannot. The mining conditions are so dangerous and severe that there is a high mortality rate. Kidnapping and abduction of men, women, and children is common, and some as young as 8 years old, are forced to serve as bodyguards, laborers, porters, domestic servants, combatants, and sex slaves.

In the CAR, the US Department of State reports that the scope of the trafficking problem is unknown. Anarchy and violence within the country due to conflicts among various armed groups have resulted in the suspension of human rights organizations ability to survey the problem. A similar condition occurs in parts of the Congo due to rogue elements of government forces, rebel and militia groups independent of the government, as well as tribal lawlessness. The mines of eastern Congo are run by multiple armed groups that vie for territory in order to capture and enslave the men, women, and children of the villages that come under their control.[17]

Various armed groups enlist children as soldiers, forcing them to participate in the violent clashes with opposing groups.

The DRC is estimated to have 873,100 slaves out of a population of

77.2 million. This ranks the country tied for 6th in the world in terms of percentage of the population in slavery according to the Walk Free Foundation's 2016 Global Slavery Index. CAR is also ranked 6th on the Prevalence Scale at 1.13 percent of the population with 55,400 slaves.

WEST AFRICA
Cote d'Ivoire

YOUSSOUF MALÉ WAS 14 AND lived in a poor village in southern Mali. Promised work in the Ivory Coast, Youssouf was kidnapped and sold to a cocoa farmer for $45, including a payoff of local police. Youssouf was told that after a year of free labor, and after he had paid back his transportation cost, he would be paid a monthly salary of ten dollars. He slept in a mud hut with eleven other slaves, working sunrise to sunset every day except for Fridays, when Youssouf would walk to another farm for low-paying work while his Muslim owner observed the Muslim day of rest.

Youssouf is a modern-day slave. (This story was published in the *New York Times Magazine* on November 18, 2001, in an article by Michael Finkel,[18] who later acknowledged it was meant to reflect an average and typical slave situation in the country and that Youssouf was not the actual person in the story.)

The Ivory Coast (Cote d'Ivoire) is located on the coast of West Africa in the Gulf of Guinea. Cote d'Ivoire received its independence from French colonial rule in 1960. It is a republic with a constitution and democratic elections. However, social and political unrest and armed conflict has adversely impacted economic development. The Ivory Coast is the world's largest producer of cocoa, the bean from which chocolate is derived. The cocoa tree originated in South America and was brought to Spain by Cortez and then introduced to Africa. The country's economy depends almost entirely on agriculture—two-thirds of the population is employed in agriculture-related labor. Labor is the principal input cost and the growing of cocoa is labor intensive. Weed control is essential and the harvesting is done by hand. It is therefore not surprising that some 90 percent of the cocoa farms use forced or slave labor. On average, cocoa farmers earn less than $2 a day, resulting in the use of child labor to keep their prices competitive.

The Ivory Coast, as poor as it is, is economically better off than its neighbors. Thus, there is a constant flow of immigrants seeking better opportunities for employment than what are available in their home countries of Burkina Faso, Mali, and Ghana. Impoverished families sell their children into slavery to work on the cocoa farms. Individuals seeking work are tricked or coerced into taking a job which turns into forced labor or actual slavery. As the immigrants head toward the Ivory Coast, they fall prey to traffickers that promise them jobs. The traffickers sell the individuals to the farmers. The worker is often unsuspecting, since he or she is illiterate, uneducated, poor, and cannot speak the local language. Once on the farm, the worker becomes a form of debtor slave as he must work to pay off his or her purchase price and earn the food, clothing, and shelter that the farmer provides. The working conditions are horrendous and slaves have little food or water. Workers may or may not be paid. They are told they will be killed if they try to escape. By breaking the spirit and will of the workers, their masters enslave them.

Cote d'Ivoire ranks 199th in the world in GDP per capita, and its economy is greatly influenced by weather and fluctuations in international prices for cocoa beans, coffee, and palm oil.[19]

The Walk Free Foundation's Global Slavery Index estimates the country has 144,900 slaves out of a population of about 22.7 million. Not surprisingly, most slaves in Cote d'Ivoire are forced to labor in agricultural fields, many of them young boys from other West African countries. Similarly, young women and girls trafficked from elsewhere in West Africa are subjected to forced labor both in the fields and, more commonly, as domestic workers, as waitresses, and in forced prostitution. In fewer cases, Ivorian women are transported to France and Saudi

Arabia as forced domestic servants.[20]

The US State Department reports that "trafficking within the country is more prevalent than transnational trafficking," and that the vast majority of trafficking victims in Cote d'Ivoire are women and children.

The State Department says that while the government of Cote d'Ivoire does not fully comply with the minimum standards for the elimination of trafficking, it is making significant efforts to do so. It is given a Tier 2 Watch List ranking.[21]

The CNN Freedom Project sent a team of journalists into the Ivory Coast to investigate child labor, trafficking, and slavery in the Ivory Coast. They found that all three conditions were rife in the cocoa agriculture.

> Chocolate's billion-dollar industry starts with workers like Abdul. He squats with a gang of a dozen harvesters on an Ivory Coast farm.
>
> Abdul holds the yellow cocoa pod lengthwise and gives it two quick cracks, snapping it open to reveal milky white cocoa beans. He dumps the beans on a growing pile.
>
> Abdul is 10 years old, a three-year veteran on the job. He has never tasted chocolate....
>
> When Abdul's mother died, a stranger brought him across the border to the farm. Abdul says all he's given is a little food, the torn clothes on his back, and an occasional tip from the farmer. Abdul is a modern child slave.
>
> And he is not the only youngster working in his group.
>
> Yacou insisted he is 16, but his face looks far younger.
>
> "My mother brought me from Burkina Faso when my father died," he said....

"I wish I could go to school. I want to read and write," he said. But Yacou hasn't spent a single day in school, and he has no idea how to leave the farm.[22]

Abdul and Yacou are modern-day slaves.

The US Department of State's 2016 Trafficking in Persons Report states:

> Cote d'Ivoire is a source, transit, and destination country for women and children subjected to forced labor and sex trafficking.... Ivoirian women and girls are primarily subjected to forced labor in domestic service and restaurants in Cote d'Ivoire but are also exploited in sex trafficking. Ivoirian boys are subjected to forced labor within the country in the agricultural and service industries, especially cocoa production.[23]

Mauritania

ABDEL NASSER OULD YESSA IS an Arab Mauritanian who was born into a slave-owning family. He owned his first slave at age seven. He later became an abolitionist and co-founded S.O.S. Slaves, an NGO human rights group. His narrative appears in the book *Enslaved*:

> Our caste system is over a thousand years old and very rigid. Master and slave see their positions as part of life's natural order. Slaves are born to one family, and stay there.... Slaves keep our camp functioning, performing all household chores, minding children, massaging the feet of their masters. They work twenty-four hours a day, seven days a week, with no time off except the day of their marriage—if they are lucky. At all times, they have to stay within earshot, to come running the instant their master beckons.[24]

Abdel's family's slaves are modern-day slaves.

Like Cote d'Ivoire, the West African country of Mauritania gained independence from French colonial rule in 1960. Mauritanian is an

Islamic republic governed under a constitution that combines French civil law and Islamic Sharia law. Its current GDP per capita, $2,200, ranks it 190th in the world, and roughly 20 percent of its citizens live on less than $1.25 a day. Three-quarters of Mauritania is desert or semi-desert. An estimated 80 percent of Mauritanians are nomadic, most working as subsistence farmers or in Mauritania's mineral resources sector.

There is a great discrepancy in the estimated number of slaves in Mauritania. A March 16, 2012 report by CNN estimated that 10–20 percent of the population lives in slavery.[25] The report estimated the slave population between 340,000 and 680,000.

According to the 2016 Global Slavery Index, slavery is entrenched in Mauritanian society, and its prevalence is perpetuated by tradition. They estimate that of 4 million citizens, 43,000 are trapped in modern slavery. In 2014, The Global Slavery Index estimated Mauritania's slavery population at 155,600. The reason for the lower estimate was not because the slave population had declined but due to the higher level of rigor in random sample surveys. This rather dramatic shift in estimate highlights the difficulty of the investigative process in countries with nomadic populations. A large portion of the Mauritanian population lives in rural areas and is nomadic. The country does not register births. Government offices keep poor records if they keep records at all. Census and surveys are poorly conducted.

Mauritania's post-colonial story is defined by the country's deeply entrenched caste system, and understanding the country's social infrastructure is vital to grasping the roots of Mauritania's modern slavery problem. The Berbers are a separate ethnic group that date back to 2000 BC and lived along the western Mediterranean coast and controlled the trans-Sahara trade routes. As Islam spread across North Africa in the seventh century, the Berbers converted to Islam brought by the Arabs. The descendants of the peoples resulting from the assimilation of the Berbers and Muslim Arabs are called Moors, and in Mauritania they are referred to as White Moors. The Islamic faith followed the Berber/Arab

Moors into Sub-Saharan Africa along the trade routes and spread to both the free as well as enslaved black Africans. The Africans that were converted to Islam in Mauritania became to be known as Black Moors.

In Mauritania today, political, cultural, and social life is controlled by the minority White Moor class. Approximately 30 percent of the population is of Arab-Berber decent, although their skin color may vary from off-white to black due to generations of genetic mixing. Throughout history, Mauritania has been a bridge between the Berbers to the north and the black Africans to the south. Indeed, Mauritania derives its name from "Moor," and is "the country of the Moors."

Mauritania suffers from a lack of government enforcement of its laws and constitution. A combination of corruption, bribes, government-owned media, favoritism based on racial, tribal, social, and political associations, and poor record-keeping promotes distrust of institutions. It is estimated that less than half of the births are recorded. Both victims and observers of female genital mutilation/cutting, torture, slavery, slavery-related practices, child labor, and trafficking are punished or killed for reporting these crimes. It is therefore difficult to place in perspective the exact extent or number of even the country's population much less the number of slaves.

The White Moors dominate the high-ranking positions in both government and business. Both the White Moors and Black Moors have maintained an Arabic culture and speak Arabic or a related dialect. There are a number of black ethnic groups that are free and have their own language and culture. In the caste social order, the offspring of Berber men and their slave mistresses are slaves. This condition is described as descent-based slavery or inherited slavery. Raised as Muslims by their Berber masters, the offspring are regarded as chattel property of their owners. They can be bought or sold, gifted, bequeathed, lent, or otherwise disposed of. They are beaten or sometimes killed. In other words, the master has control over their life and death. They experience natal alienation, violence, and dishonor.

The CNN report referenced above describes the slave system of Mauritania through an interview with a slave named Moulkheir:

> Slave masters in Mauritania exercise full ownership over their slaves. They can send them away at will, and it's common for a master to give away a young slave as a wedding present. This practice tears families apart; Moulkheir never knew her mother and barely knew her father.
>
> Most slave families in Mauritania consist of dark-skinned people whose ancestors were captured by lighter-skinned Arab Berbers centuries ago. Slaves typically are not bought and sold—only given as gifts, and bound for life. Their offspring automatically become slaves, too.
>
> All of Moulkheir's children were born into slavery.
>
> And all were the result of rape by her master.
>
> The attacks began when she had barely begun to cover her head with a scarf, a Muslim tradition that begins at puberty. The master took Moulkheir out to the goat fields near his home and raped her in front of the animals. Moulkheir had no choice but to endure this torture. She'd convinced herself that her master knew what was best for her—that this was the way it had always been, would always be.
>
> She couldn't see beyond her small, enslaved world.[26]

All of Moulkheir's children were born into slavery and are modern-day slaves.

The United States Department of State, in its 2013 report on human rights practices in Mauritania, makes the following observations:

> Slavery-like practices, typically flowing from ancestral master-slave relationships and involving both adults and children,

continued.... Such practices occurred primarily in areas where educational levels were generally low or a barter economy still prevailed, and in urban centers, including Nouakchott, where slavery-like domestic service existed. The practices commonly occurred where there was a need for workers to herd livestock, tend fields, and do other manual labor. Some former slaves and descendants of slaves were forced to work for their old masters in exchange for some combination of lodging, food, and medical care. Individuals in subservient circumstances were vulnerable to mistreatment. Women with children faced particular difficulties and could be compelled to remain in a condition of servitude, performing domestic duties, tending fields, or herding animals without remuneration....

Forced labor also occurred in urban centers where young children, often girls, were retained as unpaid household servants.[27]

Not surprisingly, in a 2014 report the US Department of State named Mauritania a Tier 3 nation because, while "the government took steps to raise public awareness about the dangers of human trafficking," the government "failed to hold traffickers criminally accountable," and in some cases, law enforcement and judicial personnel even "intervened on behalf of alleged offenders to thwart the progress of criminal prosecutions." While the Mauritanian government founded a National Agency to Fight against the Vestiges of Slavery, Integration, and Fight against Poverty (known domestically as Tadamoun), the agency has yet to submit a single complaint on behalf of a victim. Finally, the State Department found that "the government did not provide adequate protective services to victims or ensure their referral to service providers to receive care, and it failed to establish procedures for the proactive identification of victims among persons arrested for prostitution and individuals detained and deported for immigration violations."[28]

Niger

ANY ADVANTAGE IMPLIED BY NIGER'S status as West Africa's largest land country is negated by the fact that the dry Sahara covers 80 percent of its land area. Named after the Niger River, Niger became independent from France in 1960, and the common and extended droughts that plague the Sahel Valley have made Niger's agrarian and subsistence-based economy one of the world's weakest.[29] Niger today is one of the poorest countries in the world. It has a history of political unrest, with multi-party elections followed by military takeovers.

Over the period of the rise and fall of the ancient Kingdoms and Empires of Ghana, Mali, and Songhai that preceded most of modern-day Niger and covering in excess of fifteen hundred years, a vigorous trade between north and south occurred. In particular, cloth from Europe, salt from the Sahara mines, horses from Arabia and weapons and firearms from the north were traded for gold, ivory, skins, slaves, handcrafts, and kola nuts from the south. Niger played a vital role in these Sub-Saharan trade routes.

There are numerous references to slavery of Africans by Africans by Arab and Berber explorers in the thirteenth through fifteenth centuries. Among the most prominent were Leo Africanus (ca. 1494–1554) and Ibn Battuta (1304–1369), who inscribed their observations as eye witnesses to the slavery that existed at the time:

> No one lives at Taghaza except the slaves of the Massufa tribe, who dig for the salt, they subsist on dates imported from Dar'a and Sijilmasa, camels flesh, and millet imported from the Negrolands. The sultan is preceded by his musicians, who carry gold and silver gumbris (two-stringed guitars), and behind him come 300 armed slaves.[30]

This above observation by Ibn Battuta preceded the African Atlantic slave trade to the New World by over one hundred and fifty years.

Ibn Battuta also noted that slaves were used in the military and as porters, household servants, and concubines. When he began his return to Morocco from Sub-Saharan Africa, his caravan included six hundred women slaves.

Much like in Mauritania, a caste system between dominant Berbers and subjected natives persists today. Particularly in the northern part of Niger, caste-based slavery continues. The 2016 Global Slavery Index estimates that 127,000 of Niger's 18.8 million citizens (0.638 percent) are held in slavery.[31] However, a June 2005 ABC News team reported that some 800,000 traditional slaves exist in Niger, amounting to about five percent of the population. An August 22, 2014, report by Deutsche Welle, Germany's international broadcaster, offers an estimate of 800,000 by Almansour Galissoune, a volunteer for Timidria, a human rights organization that works with Anti-Slavery International. Obviously, it is difficult to estimate the number of slaves in Niger.

There are three types of slaves in Niger. The first is chattel slaves who are owned by their masters just as they own the livestock they control. These slaves are born into the bottom of the social order. The second type is former slaves who still pay tribute to their former masters in the form of crops or money, a condition of forced labor. These are called *harratines*, meaning freed slaves, but because of their continued form of servitude, they are held in low esteem. The third type of slavery is the sale of young girls by one master to another for household work and as "fifth wives" for sexual service. This practice is called *wahaya* and the victims are referred to as *wahaya*.

Tikirit Amoudar was sold to a husband through *wahaya*:

I became a *wahaya* when I was 10, and I lived as one for 15 years.

My master, a man called Amola Zono, lived in his family village.... I was his only *wahaya* and my clothes set me apart from his four legal wives. They dressed decently, while my clothes

72

barely covered me. He used to come to me at night in secret for sex. My workload was heavy: fetching water for all the family; fetching water for livestock (over 100 cattle); hulling and pounding grain (millet and sorghum) for food and foodstuffs; providing firewood for the family; large preparations—the day before and on the days of community gatherings in the master's fields during the rainy season (for 30 to 40 people); washing up; preparing the mistresses' and master's beds; looking after the children and keeping the courtyard clean—these were my tasks until my master's death in 1988.

... I could never make any suggestions; I was just a "thing," a multi-purpose object to be used at any time, however and whenever.[32]

Amoudar is a modern-day slave.

According to the US Department of State, Niger children are still routinely forced into labor in the country's gold mines, agriculture, and stone quarries.[33]

According to the State Department, Niger is a source, transit, and destination country for children, women, and men subjected to forced labor and sex trafficking. Caste-based slavery practices continue primarily in the northern part of the country.

The State Department notes that the Government of Niger is making significant efforts to comply with the minimum standards for the elimination of trafficking. In an important first step, Niger criminalized slavery for the first time in 2003. In 2014, the National Agency for the Fight Against Trafficking in Persons was established as a permanent organization to fight slavery and sex trafficking in Niger.[34] In June of 2014, the first-ever conviction of a man for slavery occurred. He was convicted for enslaving a girl as a fifth wife.[35] However, it is clear that Niger's battle against human trafficking is an uphill one, particularly considering the country's weak governmental infrastructure and lack of bureaucratic control and the rule of law. In 2016 the US State Department gave the country a Tier 2 Watch List ranking.

Nigeria

WITH AN ESTIMATED POPULATION OF 182 million, Nigeria is the most populous country in Africa. Nigeria gained independence from British colonial rule in 1960, and modern-day Nigeria is best understood as a bifurcation of the Muslim north (Islam was introduced to the area in the eighth century by Berber and Moor traders) and the Christian south (by Christian missionaries establishing British educational institutions in the colonial nineteenth century). While Nigeria is technically a secular democratic government, its history is one of military dictatorships and democratically elected civilian officials. It has the largest economy in Africa.[36]

The Niger and Benin Rivers that converge in the middle of Nigeria played a significant role in the main trade routes between Northern and Southern Africa for centuries. As in Niger, this included a booming slave trade predating both Arab and British influence, exacerbated by the country's legacy of ethnic and religious tension that continues today.

Of Nigeria's 182 million citizens, an estimated 875,500 (0.48 percent) live in slavery today. This total number is the eighth largest in the world.[37] A June 2005 ABC News team reported that some 800,000 traditional slaves exist in Niger, amounting to about 5 percent of the population. An August 22, 2014, report by Deutsche Welle, offered an estimate of 800,000, again by Almansour Galissoune, referred to earlier.

According to the US State Department's most recent Trafficking in Persons Report, Nigerian trafficking victims are recruited from rural and, to a lesser extent, urban areas within the country: women and girls for domestic servitude and sex trafficking, and boys for forced labor in street vending, domestic service, mining, stone quarrying, agriculture, and begging. Nigerian women are some of the most exploited of any population in the modern sex slavery epidemic. Reports of Nigerian women in prostitution range from Spain, Scotland, the Netherlands, Germany, Turkey, Belgium, Denmark, Finland, France, Sweden, Switzerland, Norway, Ireland, Slovakia, Greece, and Russia.[38]

> Authorities in Nigeria say as many as 40,000 girls and women have been trafficked to nearby West African countries to serve as sex workers. Simon Egede said Wednesday that investigators from his National Agency for Prohibition of Traffic in Persons found slave camps full of Nigerian women and girls in Mali, Ivory Coast, Burkina Faso, Niger, Libya, Morocco, and Cape Verde. He says he estimates that there are between 20,000 and 40,000 victims. He says Malian officials are planning arrests soon, and that Nigerian authorities are working to shut down operations elsewhere and prosecute the Nigerian traffickers.[39]

Thus, according to the US State Department, Nigeria is a source, transit, and destination country for children, women, and men subjected to forced labor and sex trafficking. Caste-based slavery practices continue primarily in the northern part of the country.

Most recently, the Islamist terrorist organization Boko Haram has ravaged northern Nigeria and kidnapped children as young as 12 to use as child soldiers and prostitutes. The organization's leader, Abubakar Shekau, is quoted saying that he would take young girls and "sell them in the market, by Allah.... We would marry them out at the age of 9. We would marry them out at the age of 12."[40]

Between 2013 and 2016 Boko Haram has kidnapped more than 10,000 boys and trained them to become child soldiers.[41]

Idriss was kidnapped by Boko Haram when he was 13 years old. At the age of 15 he was teaching other captives as young as 5 on how to handle assault rifles and become child soldiers and wage jihad holy war. "I was terrified if I didn't do it, they would kill me." Another captive, Samiyu, stated, "They told us, 'It's all right for you to kill and slaughter even your parents.... This is what you have to do to get to heaven.'"[42]

Idriss and Samiyu are modern-day slaves.

Nigeria is home to baby factories where women and girls, both pregnant or not, are held to produce babies which are then sold by traffickers.

> Neighbours were suspicious of the daytime silence at the maternity clinic that came to life only after nightfall, though never suspected its disquieting secret—it was breeding babies for sale.

> But recent police raids have revealed an alleged network of such clinics, dubbed baby "farms" or "factories" in the local press, forcing a new look at the scope of people trafficking in Nigeria....

> The doctor in charge, who is now on trial, reportedly lured teenagers with unwanted pregnancies by offering to help with abortion.

> They would be locked up there until they gave birth, whereupon they would be forced to give up their babies for a token fee of around 20,000 naira ($170).

> The babies would then be sold to buyers for anything between 300,000 and 450,000 naira ($2,500 and $3,800) each, according to a state agency fighting human trafficking in Nigeria, the National Agency for the Prohibition of Trafficking in Persons (Naptip).[43]

The US State Department Report on Human Rights confirms the preceding article:

> So-called baby factories, small facilities disguised as private medical clinics, housed pregnant women, mostly young unmarried girls, and offered their children for sale. In some cases young women were held against their will and raped, with their newborns sold on the black market for several thousand dol-

lars, with boys fetching higher prices. The children were sold for various purposes, including adoption, child labor, prostitution, or sacrificial rituals.[44]

The US State Department deems Nigeria a Tier 3 trafficking country but reports that the government is making significant strides to improve. The country's National Agency for the Prohibition of Trafficking in Persons continues to increase its efforts to identify and provide services to victims, and the government increased the number of trafficking investigations and now provides anti-trafficking training to government officials in a growing number of ministries and agencies. However, the government has yet to pass legislation to require prison time for sentenced traffickers and has not implemented formal procedures for the return and reintegration of Nigerians sold into slavery abroad.[45]

EAST AFRICA

OF THE 46 MILLION PEOPLE living in slavery around the globe today, close to one million are in East Africa. Long-term conflict, extreme poverty, corruption, government ineffectiveness, and economic dependence on valuable natural resources like oil and diamonds make East African nations particularly susceptible to cyclical slavery.[46] With the exception of Somalia, these governments are reasonably stable, with mostly secular constitutional governments and semi-democratic to democratic institutions. All of them experienced some form of colonial rule from the late nineteenth century through the aftermath of World War II.

East Africa includes Tanzania, Kenya, Uganda, Rwanda, Burundi, Ethiopia, and Somalia, the latter two, along with Djibouti and Eritrea, are also known as the Horn of Africa. South Sudan is sometimes also considered part of East Africa, but that country is addressed in another section.

Kenya, Uganda, and Ethiopia are ranked Tier 2 countries by the 2016 Trafficking in Persons Report because they do not meet the minimum standards for efforts to address human trafficking but are making efforts to do so. The Walk Free Foundation's Global Slavery Index estimates 244,400 slaves in Uganda, 0.626 percent of a population of 39 million, and 188,800 enslaved in Kenya, 0.041 percent of the population of 46 million. Ethiopia has 411,600 slaves according to the Index. Rwanda and Tanzania are given a Tier 2 Watch List ranking because they have not provided evidence to combat severe forms of human trafficking among other deficiencies. Each country, respectively, has 74,100 and 341,400 people enslaved, according to the Index. Somalia is ranked as a special case because of internal civil strife, but the Index estimates it has 121,900 enslaved, or 1.13 percent of a population of 10.8 million, placing Somalia in a tie for 6th in the world as to the prevalence of slavery.

The United States Department of State report of 2016 concludes that all of East Africa remains a source, transit, and destination for trafficked people. Children as young as seven are forced into labor in agriculture, cattle herding, mining, stone quarrying, brick making, car washing, scrap metal collecting, bars, restaurants, and the domestic service industries. Girls and boys are also forced into the sex trade as prostitutes.

East Africa's documented history of slavery dates back at least thirteen hundred years, well before the first European contact in the fourteenth century. There are reports of East African slaves captured by Arab traders bound for Asia and the Middle East as early as the eighth century.

In AD 785, the Chinese began to trade directly with East Africa in order to bypass Arab merchants. In AD 863, Chinese writer and explorer Tuan Ch'eng-shih wrote an account of the East African trade in ivory, ambergris, and slaves:

> The country of the Po-pa-li (Somalia) is in the southwestern sea. (The people) do not eat any of the five grains but eat only meat. They often stick a needle into the veins of cattle and draw

blood which they drink raw, mixed with milk. They wear no cloths except that they cover (the parts) below their loins with sheepskins. Their women are clean and of proper behaviour. The inhabitants themselves kidnap them, and if they sell them to foreign merchants, they fetch several times their price. The country produces only ivory and ambergris. If Persian merchants wish to go into their country, they collect around them several thousand men and present them with strips of cloth. All, whether old or young, draw blood and swear an oath, and then only do they trade their products. From olden times they were not subject to any foreign country. In fighting they use elephants' tusks and ribs and the horns of wild buffaloes as lances and they wear cuirasses and bows and arrows. They have twenty myriads of foot soldiers. The Arabs make frequent raids upon them.[47]

Slaves from East Africa, called Zanj, were transported to the confluence of the Tigris and Euphrates Rivers in Mesopotamia, modern day Iraq, for use in draining the marshlands and swamps and building canals. In AD 869, these slaves rebelled in what many scholars believe to be one of the largest slave revolts in history. The six-year Zanj slave revolt involved some 500,000 slaves. If this number is correct, it attests to the magnitude of the slave trade between East Africa and the Middle East. Given the harshness of the work and the prevalence of disease, particularly malaria, this slave trade had to have occurred over many years and in relatively large numbers given what we know of the sailing ships in use at the time.[48]

Another Chinese traveler, Chou Ch'u-fer, describes the slave trade in East Africa in AD 1178.

> ...there is an island in the sea on which there are many savages. Their bodies are black as lacquer and they have frizzled hair. They are enticed by food and then captured and sold as slaves

to the Arabic countries, where they fetch a very high price. They are employed as gate-keepers, and it is said that they have no longing for their kinfolk…thousands of them are sold as foreign slaves.[49]

Myriad references to a steady supply of black Africans from East Africa to China during the reign of Emperor Chien-wen of China from 1399 to 1402 demonstrate the extent to which African slavery spread to the east more than a century before the advent of the Atlantic slave trade.

In Kuang-chou most of the wealthy people keep devil-slaves. They are very strong and can lift weights of several hundred catties. Their language and tastes are unintelligible. Their nature is simple and they do not run away. They are also called "wildmen." Their color is black as ink, their lips are red and their teeth white. The people of Chan-ch'eng (Champa) buy male and female slaves; the ships carry human beings as cargo.[50]

Islam forbids the enslavement of fellow Muslims. As is true now and has been true since the beginning of time, what is forbidden by law or scripture is often permitted in real life. The Arabs are white and the Sub-Saharan Africans are black. The Arabs have been enslaving black Africans since before Islam and before the Europeans had contact with Africa. Today, Muslims enslave fellow Muslims in Africa, the Middle East, and Asia. Tradition and culture trump religion. For example, in Mende's case, she realized that her captors were Muslims:

But the more I thought about it the more I realized that all my oppressors had been Muslims. The raiders had all shout-ed, "Allahu Akhdar," when they had attacked our village. The slave trader Abdul Azzim had also been a Muslim. And now Rahab and her family. All these people believed themselves to

80

be good Muslims. Yet they had killed and raped and tortured and enslaved the Nuba people from my tribe—who were all Muslims too.[51]

The eastern African slave trade that involved the Sahara, the Red Sea, and the Indian Ocean has not gained the same attention as the Atlantic slave trade. One estimate is that over the past fourteen centuries some twenty-eight million Africans were enslaved into the Arab/Muslim world of the Middle East, Eurasia, and Asia and that the number of victims of this slave trade could exceed one hundred and eighty million. The contrast between the American and Middle East slave trades is startling. The slaves shipped to the Americas were used primarily for agriculture, while those taken to the Arab/Muslim countries were used as concubines, in harems, and in military service. About 10–15 percent of the Atlantic trade perished on the Atlantic crossing, while those slaves transiting the Sahara and the eastern seas had a mortality rate of 80–90 percent. Two-thirds of the slaves in the Atlantic slave trade were men while two-thirds of the Arab trade were women. Many of the one-third of the African men destined to the Arab/Muslim world were castrated eunuchs. Once the slaves reached their destinations, many more of those in the Americas survived and their descendants are citizens of their respective nations, very few of the descendants of the Arab/Muslim slave trade to the Middle East, Eurasia, and Near East have survived to the current period in the Muslim world. The Western world initiated its abolition movement to free its African slaves, no such abolition movement developed in the Arab/Muslim world of the Middle East, Eurasia, and Asia.[52]

CHAPTER FIVE

Asia

NORTH KOREA

SHIN DONG-HYUK IS THOUGHT TO be the only person to be born in a North Korean labor camp to have escaped. He was born in Camp 14 in 1982 and in 2005, at age 24, escaped. He made his way to China and in 2006 entered South Korea. He lived in the United States for several years and then returned to South Korea, where he is a human rights proponent. He told his story to Blaine Harden, an author and journalist, who wrote the biography *Escape from Camp 14*, published in 2012. Shin witnessed his first execution in Camp 14 at the age of four. At age fourteen, he witnessed the execution of his mother and brother. Harden, the author, describes Shin's experience:

> His mother beat him, and he viewed her as a competitor for food. His father, who was allowed by guards to sleep with his mother just five nights a year, ignored him. His brother was a stranger. Children in the camp were untrustworthy and abusive. Before he learned anything else, Shin learned to survive by snitching on all of them.... Love and mercy and family were words without meaning. God did not disappear or die. Shin had never heard of him.[1]

In an interview at a human rights summit in Geneva in 2013, Shin stated that the prison camps were like the Holocaust. Shin stated, "The birth of a baby is a blessed thing in the outside world, but inside the camp, babies are born to be slaves like their parents. It's an absolute scandal."[2] Another North Korean camp survivor quoted in the article, Chol-Hwan Kang, likens the camps in North Korea to Auschwitz, the notorious extermination facility for Jews run by Hitler's Germany during World War II:

> "Fundamentally, it is the same as Hitler's Auschwitz." With whole families in North Korea thrown into camps together and starving to death, he said "the methods may be different, but the effect is the same.... It's outrageous!"[3]

An article by Tom Blackwell in the *National Post* describes life inside one of the camps. He had the opportunity to interview an escaped prisoner as well as a former guard at the camp. An Myeong Chul worked in the camp as a guard for eight years, and sensing that he and his family were about to be thrown into the camp for a made-up violation, they fled. He is quoted in the article:

> "If we were to help these prisoners in any way or be compassionate, we would be executed and our families as well, and we were given the right to kill any prisoner who attempted to escape," he said. "I remember a colleague dragging a prisoner who was working in the field and executing this prisoner."

> Mr. An said he witnessed "a lot of deaths" of inmates, whether as a result of violence by camp authorities, starvation, overwork or accidents in workplaces like the coal mine where prisoners toiled at the notorious Camp 22.

> "The best way to put it is they were the slaves, and we were the slave owners."[4]

North Korea, Democratic People's Republic of Korea (DPRK), is a totalitarian dictatorship located on the Korean Peninsula in East Asia. At the conclusion of World War Two, the Korean Peninsula was divided between two separate governments, the other being South Korea. North Korea is perhaps the world's most repressive régime, and according to the 2016 Global Slavery Index, no country has done less to address its problems of modern slavery. In fact, North Korea is the only country in the world that does not have a national law criminalizing any form of modern slavery.

According to the Global Slavery Index, approximately 1.1 million North Koreans (4.37 percent of the country's population of 25.2 million) live in modern-day slavery. The majority of these people are held in forced labor camps as both political prisoners and other undesirables as deemed by the state. The Global Slavery Index lists North Korea's population as the world's most at risk to worsening modern slavery conditions due to "government sanctioned forced labor, a dramatic absence of human rights provisions, and high levels of poverty."

These camps began in the 1950s to punish political prisoners; in 1972, Kim Il Sung, the dictator, decreed that "enemies of class, whoever they are, their seed must be eliminated through three generations."[5]

Those in forced labor camps live in desperate conditions. According to the 2014 UN Report of the Commission of Inquiry on Human Rights in the Democratic People's Republic of Korea, "prisoners in the ordinary prison system are systematically subjected to deliberate starvation and illegal forced labor."[6] Many are forced to work 12 to 15 hour days for no pay and with no days off. They are issued a set of clothes once or twice a year and are not issued underclothes, socks, gloves, toilet paper, or toothbrushes. Several people are executed in ceremonial events each year. Others are beaten to death and raped by guards at will. The forced labor is directed to farming, mining, logging, garment and uniform manufacture, and cement production, and prisoners must meet daily production quotas or they are beaten and their food rations are reduced. Their diet consists of corn, cabbage, and salt. The inmates usually die from malnutrition or malnutrition-related diseases. Those responsible for their imprisonment have never been charged with a crime or prosecuted, convicted, or sentenced by any kind of impartial trial.[7]

The North Korean government sends its citizens to foreign countries under work contracts where they are employed in logging, construction, and farming. The workers' wages are deposited to government accounts. The workers are assigned jobs that they are forced to undertake with the threat of beatings or killings if they do not comply. Threats of reprisals to their families back home encourage the workers to submit to the forced labor contracts. North Korean "overseers" treat the workers as slaves in that the laborers have no choice of the work they do, receive little or no wages, are housed in penitentiary-like conditions, and their movements and communications are monitored. They are punished if they do not meet production quotas. The United States Department of State estimates that thousands of North Korean laborers are under such contracts in Russia and China.

North Korea also has a well-established system of raiding, kidnapping, and abducting citizens of other countries and bringing them back to North Korea and forcing them to work in various occupations for little or no money. They are threatened with severe punishment or death if they try to escape. According to the US Department of State in its 2016 Trafficking in Persons Report, "political prisoners are subjected to unhygienic living conditions, beatings, torture, rape, a lack of medical care, and insufficient food. Many prisoners do not survive. Furnaces and mass graves are used to dispose the bodies of those who die in these prison camps."[8]

The United Nations' Commission of Inquiry on Human Rights in the DPRK reports:

> North Korea is a state that does not content itself with ensuring the authoritarian rule of a small group of people, but seeks to dominate every aspect of its citizens' lives and terrorizes them from within.[9]

A press release announcing publication of the commission's findings states:

> These crimes against humanity entail extermination, murder, enslavement, torture, imprisonment, rape, forced abortions and other sexual violence, persecution on political, religious, racial and gender grounds, the forcible transfer of populations, the enforced disappearance of persons and the inhumane act of knowingly causing prolonged starvation....Violations of the rights to food and to freedom of movement have resulted in women and girls becoming vulnerable to trafficking and forced sex work outside the DPRK. Many take the risk of fleeing, mainly to China, despite the high chance that they will be apprehended and forcibly repatriated, then subjected to persecution, torture, prolonged arbitrary detention and, in some cases, sexual violence. "Repatriated women who are pregnant are regularly subjected to forced abortions, and babies born to repatriated women are often killed," the report states.
>
> The Commission also found that, since 1950, the "State's violence has been externalized through State-sponsored abductions and enforced disappearances of people from other nations. These international enforced disappearances are unique in their intensity, scale and nature."[10]

Not surprisingly, in 2016 North Korea received a Tier 3 ranking from the United States Department of State because the country does not meet the minimum standards, and is not making significant efforts, to comply with the Trafficking Victims Protection Act.

PAKISTAN

RANJHAN IS A DEBTOR SLAVE in a brick factory in Pakistan, and his story is typical of victims who initially borrow money from employers. A father of three, Ranjhan labors seven days a week at the coal-fired kiln.

> I borrowed 40,000–50,000 rupees (£413–516) to buy food for my children. I will never pay it back before I die—my debt will not die with me.

His employer keeps his wages to repay the loan, but the wages do not cover the loan or interest charged, so his debt increases every month. He is paid about $1.50 for every 1,000 bricks he produces.[11]

Ranjhan is a modern-day slave.

Pakistan is in South Asia and is bordered by the Arabian Sea and the Gulf of Oman in the south, India to the east, Afghanistan to the west, Iran to the southwest, and China in the northeast.

The modern state of Pakistan was established in 1947 with the partition of British India into the two states of India and Pakistan. The partition led to millions of Muslims relocating to Pakistan while millions of Hindus and Sikhs moved to India. In 1971, East Pakistan broke with Pakistan to become the independent state of Bangladesh.

Pakistan is technically a federal parliamentary republic, but its history is one of political instability, including military rule intertwined with democratic elections. It has the sixth largest population in the world, with approximately 188 million, but its gross national product of approximately $225 billion and per capita GDP of approximately $2,800 rank 45th and 147th respectively, placing the country economically in the non-developed and emerging market category. Its economy is about the same size as Chile and Egypt.

According to the 2016 Global Slavery Index, Pakistan's population suffers from the world's sixth highest prevalence of modern slavery. Currently, 2.134 million Pakistanis (1.13 percent of the country's population) live in slavery.

Nowhere in the world is debt bondage more prevalent than Pakistan. Much of Pakistan's worker population toils under the *hari* system, in which laborers are required to hand over their entire yield to their employers and are paid only in what they produce. In order to survive, laborers must borrow money from their landlords, creating a spiral of poverty, debt, and entrapping families for generations. For example, the brick kiln industry alone employs roughly 4.5 million people in Pakistan, and the vast majority of brick kiln workers are considered unregistered bonded laborers.

Kashif Bajeer, secretary of Pakistan's National Coalition Against Bonded Labor, estimates that 70 percent of the bonded labor in the country are children and places the total number of debtor slaves in Pakistan at eight million. Many families live in impoverished regions and do not register births. Without a birth registration, the family and baby do not receive a national ID card. Without a national ID card, one cannot vote. This shields local officials from accountability for not enforcing the laws against slavery and protects the employers who in turn bribe local law enforcement.[12]

Debt bondage exists in brick kiln factories, agriculture, carpet weaving and knotting, construction, and other forms of production. The Supplementary Convention on the Abolition of Slavery, the Slave Trade, and Institutions and Practices Similar to Slavery defines debt bondage (debt slavery, bonded labor) as

> The status or condition arising from a pledge by a debtor of his personal services or of those of a person under his control as security for a debt, if the value of those services as reasonably assessed is not applied towards the liquidation of the debt or the length and nature of those services are not respectively limited and defined.[13]

These debts can be passed from one generation to another.

The Borgen Project is a human rights NGO that addresses the correlation between poverty and slavery. In a release entitled "Women and Modern Day Slavery in Pakistan," it reports:

According to *The Nation*, women in Pakistan are forced to make bricks in order to pay off the debt their families have incurred.

> "Living without running water, and often trapped by their employers for the rest of their lives, these women are forced to work in brick kilns, agricultural fields, and other hard labour industries to clear debts which overshadow their families' lives," said the Pakistani news agency.[14]

Hamo has worked as a farm laborer since he was 5 along with his twelve family members in an area outside of Hyderabad, in southern Sindh, Pakistan. He and his family have been sold from one farm to another. He, as well as his parents, has borrowed money from the farm owners, who also happen to be connected to officials in the local community. The family has never seen the landlord, only the farm manager. They are descent-based slaves since the debt that they owe the landlord and are unable to repay is passed from one generation to the next. If they leave the farm they will have no shelter or food. Additionally, since all the landlords are friends and in cooperatives together, none will hire them if they leave. There is also the threat of violence to them or their family, as well as the threat that the farm manager will sell a family member to another farm: natal alienation. While Pakistan has laws against slavery, they are not enforced and corruption is widespread.

> "There is not even a single kiln in Lahore and its suburbs which is not owned by the politicians who are sitting in corridors of power, including federal and provincial assemblies," said Ibn Abdur Rehman, a prominent human rights activist and president of the National Coalition Against Bonded Labor.[15]

It is not uncommon for Pakistani couples to sell their children in order to lighten the burden of feeding them or to pay off debt. Many hope that the children they sell will have a better life than what they could offer. However, despite the promise by the buyer (often a trafficker) of a better life for the child, the child is condemned to a life of forced labor, confinement, lack of remuneration, sexual abuse, and violence. Often the children are trafficked into the sex trade. In one report, parents were attempting to sell their children for a bag of flour. These children are illiterate and will never attend school. Despite laws that forbid bonded labor and the trafficking in adults and children, they are not enforced due to bribes and corruption among law enforcement officials.[16]

> Children as young as 5 are auctioned off regularly in a warehouse here in Pakistan's lawless border regions. Most of them are impoverished Afghan refugees bound for lives of servitude or prostitution....
>
> Girls are auctioned off in a large rectangular room about 40 feet by 30 feet where intricate Afghan carpets cover the floor and pillows serve as seats for low tables.
>
> Buyers puff on hookahs as the girls, escorted by an elderly woman, walk to a dais in the center of the room dressed only in thin cotton smocks. Before purchase, a buyer has the right to remove the tunic and inspect the girl in front of the crowd.
>
> "The selling of children is common among the poor in Pakistan and Afghanistan," said Syed Mehmood Asghar, a program manager specializing in child abuse for Save the Children Sweden, based in Peshawar. "It has always been in the culture; the poor do not regard it as slavery."[17]

Victims are reluctant to testify against their employers for fear of reprisals against themselves and their families. Gathering data is hampered by the fact that much of the country is rural, many births are unregistered, sections of the country are ungovernable, corruption is widespread, and the victims themselves are impoverished and illiterate. The survey states that debt bondage is the most prevalent form of modern slavery in Pakistan. The debt is not extinguished upon the death of the worker, but instead is transferred to other family members including children. Some bonded workers are held in captivity and their family treated as hostages. The Walk Free Foundation estimates that there are ten million child workers in Pakistan, 3.8 million of whom are five to fourteen years old. Children are used in the brick kiln factories, agriculture, domestic work, auto mechanic shops, carpet-weaving establishments, and in commercial sex and prostitution trade. They have identified the trafficking of Pakistani men and women to Europe and the Middle East for forced labor, sexual exploitation, and forced marriage.[18]

The United States Trafficking in Persons Report for 2016 ranks Pakistan as a Tier 2 Watch List country. The vast majority of the government's resources are directed toward counterterrorism and counterinsurgency efforts due to the deteriorating security situation in the region. The report states that Pakistan is a source, transit, and destination country for men, women, and children subjected to forced labor and sex trafficking.

> Children are bought, sold, rented, or kidnapped and placed in organized begging rings, domestic servitude, small shops, brick kilns, and prostitution.... Trafficking experts describe a structured system for exploiting women and girls in sex trafficking, including offering victims for sale in physical markets.[19]

A series of constitutional amendments passed in 2010 delegated many of the federal government's powers to the provinces, including responsibility for labor and the protection of child and women's protection. Provincial governments have struggled to adopt these new responsibilities, and lacking any rule of law, widespread corruption and poverty "reinforce political, social, and economic structures of modern slavery in Pakistan."[20]

INDIA

LEELU BAI WAS EXCITED TO become a bride in India, but instead she entered a life of imprisonment as she toiled to satisfy her husband's debts:

> I became bonded after I got married to my husband 20 years ago—his family had been bonded for three generations to the same landlord—they took loans for marriage, for illness, for education and so it went on ... I used to work from 6:00 am in the landlord's house—cleaning, fetching water.... Then I would go to work on the farm ... cutting, threshing and so on until 7:00 pm or later. Sometimes I would have to go back to the landlord's house to clean and wash everything. Only after I had finished could I go home to feed my family. My landlord never let me work with another landlord, he would abuse us and threaten to beat us if we ever went to work for someone else. If we were ill, the landlord would come to our houses and tell us that we were very lazy and so on.... [21]

Leelu is a modern-day slave.

Lakshmi was abducted at age 9 from her village in northeastern India and sold to a family far away in West Delhi to work as domestic help. She was rescued four years later at age 13. Her kidnappers sexually assaulted her while trafficking her to the employer. She received no wages, as the employer paid what would have been her meager salary to the trafficker. She was told that if she tried to escape, there would be reprisals back to her family in her village.

> "I was not allowed to rest," she says. "If I did something wrong or it was not what they wanted, they hit me.

> "If I wanted to sit down for a bit because I was so tired, they would scream at me. I was never allowed to leave the house, so

93

I didn't realise that I'm in Delhi. My employers told me that we are in Madras in South India."[22]

Lakshmi is a modern-day slave.

India is the largest country in southern Asia. It gained its independence from the United Kingdom in 1947, having been ruled by the British since the early eighteenth century. It is federal parliamentary constitutional republic. It has a nominal gross domestic product of about $2 trillion, ranking it tenth in the world, and a purchasing power parity GDP of about $7 trillion, ranking third behind the United States and China.

India has a population in excess of 1.3 billion people, with more than half living below the income poverty line. In order to compete in the world economy, cheap or forced labor is essential. This labor dynamic, coupled with the Indian caste system, lends itself to slavery. The untouchables and the indigenous tribal groups at the bottom of the class system and among the most impoverished of the various classes within the caste order, are the most vulnerable to being victims of slavery, particularly debtor bondage. Child debtor slavery is widespread. Poverty is the motivation for parents selling their children into slavery. Children are docile, easy to control, easily exploited, require less food, and take up less space. The child is either sold outright or is collateral for a loan. The price ranges between $14 and $214. India has up to 5 million children in debtor slavery and about 44 million workers under the age of 13. An estimated 15 to 20 million debtor slaves exist in India, Pakistan, Bangladesh, and Nepal.[23] The Walk Free Foundation in its 2016 Global Slavery Index estimates that India has 18.4 million slaves.

A study of the carpet-making industry in India by researcher Swathi Mehta found that some 300,000 children worked in this industry as slaves.[24] Their small hands are more adept at making the knots in the carpets. Ms. Mehta also found that Pakistan uses about 300,000 child slaves in its carpet-making industry, while Nepal has between 100,000 and 200,000 child slaves in its carpet industry. Other domestic and export-oriented industries in India also utilize slave labor, especially the enslavement of children. These industries include agriculture, textile manufacturing, silk production, prostitution, glass blowing, salt production, cigarette rolling, soccer ball stitching, fireworks manufacturing, and the leather industry, to mention a few. Parents often sell their children into slavery either for the money for subsistence living or to pay off a debt. Many families have numerous children, and the sale of a child results in one less mouth to feed. In many cases, children are their parents' only assets. When three billion people worldwide live on less than two dollars a day, it is not difficult to see how a child might be his or her parents' most valuable possession. Even so, in India and other parts of Asia, children are sold for less than the price of a farm animal.

The hand-knotted carpet-making industry in India is highly fragmented, with an estimated 70,000 looms in the northeastern state of Uttar Pradesh, where the industry is concentrated. Most of the looms are one-man shops in remote villages that use just a handful of children. They are not registered with the appropriate local, state, or federal governments. The source of labor for the loom-owners is the purchase of kidnapped children, the purchase of a child from a family, or a loan to the family for the services of the child. Ms. Mehta's study found that many of the children start work at age four or five. They work 12 to 18 hours a day, seven days a week. Often they are chained to their looms during the night. The looms are in small huts with no windows and poor lighting. The children are beaten, branded and, if caught trying to escape, often killed. The difficult working conditions cause injury, illness, and deformity. In Ms. Mehta's documentary, she cites the stories of several eyewitness victims. One was a case where a boy was sold into slavery for a loan of $12 so that the parents could pay for his brother's wedding. He was four years old. He was chained to the loom, worked 12 hour days, and was mentally and physically abused. He was freed after six years with the help of the Bonded Labor Liberation Front, a human rights NGO, and later became an advocate for human rights.[25] Justice P. N. Bhagwati of the Indian Supreme Court stated:

> [Bonded labourers] are non-beings, exiles of civilization, living a life worse than that of animals, for animals are at least free to roam about as they like.... This system, under which one person can be bonded to provide labour for another for years and years until an alleged debt is supposed to be wiped out, which never seems to happen during the lifetime of the bonded labourer, is totally incompatible with the new egalitarian socio-economic order which we have promised to build. [26]

A publication entitled "Slavery on the High Street: Forced Labour in the Manufacture of Garments for International Brands" by Anti-Slavery International investigated forced and child labor in India in the manufacture of fabrics and garments. The report "identifies the use of slavery-like practices involved in the manufacture of garments in India for international markets: the use of forced labour of young women and girls in the factories of Southern India, particularly the spinning mills around Tirupur. This report also identifies the routine use of child labour in garment finishing in Delhi."[27]

The report examined the supply chains of major international branded products that are in India and confirmed that young women and girls were forced to work in manufacturing facilities in Tamil Nadu. Although India has adopted new laws against child labor and forced labor, it is widespread in very rural areas where a child or adult person has been trafficked and has no knowledge of where they are or the local dialect.

The report went on to state:

> Extensive use of child labour was identified by this research in the Sangam Vihar and Tughlakabad areas of Delhi, particularly

relating to work on applying sequins, beads, embroidery, and similar finishes to garments for international markets. Despite the existence of machinery for many of these finishes, this work is generally, but not exclusively, undertaken by adolescent boys and young men aged between 10 and 20. One of the reasons that child labour is used so extensively in this part of the garment industry is because, paradoxically, of the close familial and community relationship between the workshop managers who are contracted to do the work, and the home villages of the child workers.[28]

In one workshop, the researchers found children sitting on the floor stitching sequins onto skirts for which they were paid 1/37th of the legal minimum wage for semi-skilled workers set by the government of India.

The "Sumangali system" entails unmarried females between 13 and 18 years of age who work for three years under a "contract." They work in factories that run continuously 24 hours a day, with three shifts of eight hours. The workers are paid well below the minimum wage, are not paid for overtime, and are confined to the workplace. They sleep in hostels adjacent to the mills and are generally restricted from leaving the area during the contract period. They are promised a bonus at the end of the contract, but few receive one, either because the employer reneges or the girls cannot complete the contract because of ill health.

BBC News reported on the slave-like conditions of brick kiln workers. The workers, including children as young as 4, pick and shovel clay in a wet pit, pack clay mud into molds that are then heat-hardened in a furnace by coal that has been quarried by the workers. Thousands of families travel to the area each year to work in the brick kilns for the six-month season of this enterprise. The working conditions are well below the standards acceptable to national or international human rights advocates. The bricks are used to build office buildings, factories, and other infrastructure that has contributed to India's emergence as one of the globe's fastest growing economies.

The workers are driven to this form of labor by extreme poverty. The work conditions, paltry wages, and abuse qualify these workers as modern-day slaves.

> The heat hardens mud clay into the bricks that are making modern India.
>
> Close by the air is acrid with coal soot, catching in the throat.
>
> Like a scene from a long-gone age, men and women walk in single file up and down steps as if climbing a pyramid. They strain under a load, balanced in yoke-like hods, to deliver freshly moulded bricks to the furnace....
>
> "We make 1,500 bricks a day. Only after six months will we get released."
>
> Nearby, there is a mound of coal. Woman and children squat at the edge. Most are barefoot. Two children, barely four years old, their faces smeared black, break coal by hitting pieces against each other.
>
> "All of this is against the law," says Aeshalla Krishna, a labour activist with the human rights group Prayas....
>
> The bricks are used to build offices, factories and call centres, the cityscapes of a booming economic miracle, and more and more, these buildings are used by multi-national companies with a global reach....
>
> Among many reports of abuses, labour contractors last week were accused of cutting off the hands of two workers who tried to leave their jobs.[29]

The report goes on to state that the workers, who include young girls and pregnant women, toil 12 to 15 hours a day, have meager food supplies and contaminated water.

"The scale of forced and child labour in the brick kilns of India is of epidemic proportions," says the UK's Andrew Brady. "Simply put, cheap bricks means cheap office buildings on the back of blood bricks and slave labour."[30]

Another human rights issue in India is the use of child labor for a number of activities including household help. Traffickers enter the homes of children, seeking girls, when their parents are away at work, and entice the children with candy and new clothes and the promise of more to come. Before the children know what has transpired, they are on a train with the traffickers to be sold to another trafficker, and eventually end up being bought by a couple for use as household servants. A BBC report quotes an interviewee as to how the traffickers operate:

> "Unscrupulous agents and middlemen just come into our homes when parents are away working at the tea gardens and lure young girls with new clothes and sweets. Before they know it, they are on a train to a big city at the mercy of these greedy men...."

> Kidnapped children are often forced into the sex trade. But many here feel that children are increasingly pushed into domestic labour—hidden from public view within the four walls of a home.

> The government estimates half a million children are in this position.

> At a rehabilitation home in northern Delhi run by a charity for children, Bachpan Bachao Andolan, many families have gathered.

(Bachpan Bachao Andolan is a human rights group that fights the trafficking of child labor in India. Since its founding in 1980, it has rescued more than 85,000 children.)

They are all tea workers from the northeast state of Assam and have come here searching for their missing daughters.

Helping these families find their daughters is Kailash Satyarti, the head of Bachpan Bacchao Andolan.

"This is the most ironical part of India's growth. The middle classes are demanding cheap, docile labour," he says.

"The cheapest and most vulnerable workforce is children—girls in particular. So the demand for cheap labour is contributing to trafficking of children from remote parts of India to big cities...."

"Unfortunately our child labour prohibition and regulation act is totally outdated," says Kushal Singh, head of the National Commission for Protection of Child Rights.

"It says children below the age of 14 cannot be employed in hazardous occupations. Does that mean in non-hazardous occupations a two-year-old child can be employed?"[31]

The Anti-Slavery Society, a human rights NGO, describes how trafficked children, and often adults, are lured into debt or bonded slavery. A trafficker will approach a family in a village. He will offer the family's child a job with good pay and working conditions. He promises to repatriate some portion of the wages back to the family. He even brings gifts to the family to confirm his sincerity regarding the well-being of the child and the family. The family sees this opportunity as a means for escaping their own as well as the child's poverty and low social status. In return for taking the child to this promise of good work, the trafficker gives the family a name and address of the prospective employer. The name and address are, in fact, fictitious. The trafficker then transports the child to the manager of a farm, garment maker, rug weaver, and livestock herder, or for use as domestic help. Some are sold to brothels to become prostitutes. The children, either alone or grouped with other children, typically perform work for which they receive no pay. They are locked up at night in a shed or other confinement, sexually abused, beaten, often branded, and fed at a subsistence level.

The master considers the price paid for the trafficked person to be a debt of the person trafficked. The master then charges an exorbitant interest on the debt. The master also adds food, clothing, and shelter to the debt. With little or no wages to try to pay off the accumulating debt, the individual becomes a "debtor slave."

The Anti-Slavery Society describes the experience of one child named Shankar:

> We were poked with burning cigarettes on the back and legs. If we cried for our mothers we were locked in a room without air or enough light. We were forced to work for 20 hours a day without pay. We were kept half fed and beaten up severely by our masters if we were found talking or laughing among ourselves. One night I jumped into the nearby River Ganges to kill myself to escape from this painful life. We were never allowed to go back to our parents, to our villages.[32]

Shankar is a modern-day slave.

A condition of ritual slavery exists in India. It consists of a family giving a young daughter to the religious temple in return for money or gifts. The girl is then dedicated or "married" to a deity. The deity most often referenced in this ceremony is Yellamma, the Goddess of fertility. A ceremony is performed and the dedicated girl is then sexually engaged by a member of the religious order. She thereafter is available to the priests of the religious order, and others who are associated with the religious order, for sexual service. The girls that are subjected to this practice are "married" to the Yellamma, or another mythological Goddess, at ages that range between eight and twelve and are initiated sexually either immediately or at puberty, usually by the age of 13–15. Such girls are handmaidens or slaves of the deity and available to sexual exploitation by the priests and devotees of the Goddess. The girls also participate in religious festivals as singers and dancers. Because they are "married" to a Goddess, they are precluded from participating in a normal marriage to a fellow human male. The girls are often turned out to the streets once they have aged and become less physically attractive. At this stage, they are vulnerable to sexual exploitation. These girls are typically of a lower caste, held in disrespect by the community and revert to prostitution and lives as sex slaves.

This practice, called temple prostitution, is thought to be over 2,000 years old. It is called by many names, "Devadasi" being the most common. The cult most likely originated in ancient agricultural settlements whereby the farmers were dependent upon the fertility of the soil to produce crops. The girls, by being married to the Goddess of fertility, were sacrificing their virginity to assure their fertility and the fertility of the land.

Through the evolution of indigenous pagan polytheistic religious practices, Devadasi and similar cults became embedded in early Jainism, Buddhism, and Hinduism. In southern India, the practice survives among Hindu followers. Anti-Slavery International estimates that tens of thousands of girls are subject to this form of bondage.[33]

The Guardian published an article entitled "Devadasis Are a Cursed Community":

> Parvatamma is a *devadasi*, or servant of god, as shown by the red-and-white beaded necklace around her neck. Dedicated to the goddess Yellamma when she was 10 at the temple in Saundatti, southern India, she cannot marry a mortal. When she reached puberty, the devadasi tradition dictated that her virginity was sold to the highest bidder and when she had a daughter at 14 she was sent to work in the red light district in Mumbai.
>
> The daughter of a devadasi, Parvatamma plans to dedicate her own daughter to Yellamma, a practice that is now outlawed in India....

Girls from poor families of the "untouchable," or lower, caste are "married" to Yellamma as young as four....

The devadasi system has been part of southern Indian life for many centuries. A veneer of religion covers the supply of concubines to wealthy men. Trained in classical music and dance, the devadasis lived in comfortable houses provided by a patron, usually a prominent man in the village. Their situation changed as the tradition was made illegal across India in 1988, and the temple itself has publicly distanced itself from their plight....

Now the system is seen as a means for poverty-stricken parents to unburden themselves of daughters. Though their fate was known, parents used religion to console themselves, and the money earned was shared....

BL Patil, the founder of Vimochana, an organization working towards the eradication of the devadasi system, says that although the dedication ceremonies are banned, the practice is still prevalent, as families and priests conduct them in secret. The National Commission for Women estimate that there are 48,358 Devadasis currently in India.[34]

India has a long history of slavery including chattel slavery, debt bondage, sex slavery, child slavery, and forced labor.

The Rigveda, the oldest scriptures of Hinduism, is thought to have been composed between 1500 and 1200 BC. The *Rigveda* was passed from one generation to another through oral tradition and committed to writing sometime between the fourth and sixth century AD. The *Rigveda* contains many accounts of the various gods and religious practices during this period. It also provides an insight to the historical, cultural, political, and social practices of the era. The *Rigveda* relates that slavery is a normal part of their society as tribes fought each other and captives were enslaved. According to the ancient text, most of the slaves were used in the household, although slaves were found among field hands, construction workers, and those doing menial tasks.

The caste system in India is complex and multifaceted and scholars disagree as to its rigidity, fluidity, sustainability, implementation, and origin. However, understanding this form of social stratification reinforces how entrenched slavery is in India. Generally speaking, there are four castes of stratified social hierarchy. There are also subdivisions within the castes. The Brahmans are the top of the social structure and consist of priests, professors, and the educated or learned class. Next are the Kshatriyas, comprised of rulers and warriors. Third are Vaishyas, comprised of landowners, traders, and merchants. At the bottom of the four classes are the Shudras, the laborers and those assigned to menial tasks, the commoners, and the servants and slaves. Outside of the four social castes are the untouchables (Dalits). They are subordinate to all the four castes and do work like toilet cleaning and garbage collection.

All levels of government in India are complicit in the non-enforcement of the laws against slavery because of custom and tradition and the extreme poverty which encourages families to sell a child into slavery. Police accept bribes and some even own brothels. Corrupt officials include local law enforcement, county and state officials, and even members of Parliament. Authorities also fail to enforce the laws against slavery because many of the slaves and victims are Dalit (untouchables), or of a lower caste or indigenous (tribal) community for whom the government officials have no compassion, respect, or caring.

The 2016 US Department of State's Trafficking in Persons Report on India states India is a source, destination, and transit country for men, women, and children subjected to forced labor and sex trafficking. The forced labor of an estimated 20 to 65 million citizens constitutes India's largest trafficking problem; men, women, and children in debt bondage—sometimes inherited from previous generations—are forced to work in industries such as brick kilns, rice mills, agriculture, and embroidery factories. NGOs observed that the majority of trafficking victims are recruited by agents known to them in their home villages with promises of work in urban or other rural areas. Trafficking between Indian states continues to rise due to increased mobility and growth in industries that use forced labor, such as construction, textiles, wire manufacturing for underground cables, biscuit factories, and floriculture. Thousands of unregulated work placement agencies reportedly engage in sex and labor trafficking but escape prosecution; some of these agents participate in the sexual abuse that approximately 20 percent of domestic workers reportedly experience. Placement agencies also provide child labor for domestic service, meeting a demand for cheap and docile workers and creating a group vulnerable to trafficking. Children are subjected to forced labor as factory workers, beggars, agricultural workers, and, in some rural areas of Northern India, as carpet weavers.

Experts estimate that millions of women and children are victims of sex trafficking in India. Children continue to be subjected to sex trafficking in religious pilgrimage centers and tourist destinations. Traffickers also pose as matchmakers, arranging sham marriages within India or to Gulf states, and then subject women and girls to sex trafficking.

Some Indian migrants who willingly seek work as construction workers, domestic servants, and other low-skilled laborers in the Middle East and, to a lesser extent, Afghanistan, Southeast Asia, Bhutan, the United States, Europe, Southern Africa, South America, the Caribbean, and other regions, subsequently face forced labor conditions initiated by recruitment fraud and usurious recruitment fees charged by Indian labor brokers.[35]

BANGLADESH

ROTHY WAS SOLD BY A trafficker to a brothel after being told of a good-paying job in the garment industry. She was 9 years old and forced to work as a prostitute. She has been in the sex industry for eight years and has about ten clients a day. The Tangail brothel is in the center of the Tangail district where about 900 prostitutes live. Ironically, the police station is next door.

Rothy is a modern-day slave.

Abul Kamal Azad responded to an ad in a Dhaka newspaper offering jobs as a chef in the UK. He met a trafficker (Shamsul Arefin), who promised him a high-paying job as a chef in Scotland. Indeed, the trafficker said he owned the hotel. Abul was struggling to make ends meet with his wife and young son. He was shown a work contact for 18,000 British pounds a year, an enormous amount compared to his earnings in Dhaka. However, he would have to pay for his transportation, work visas, sponsorship, and other expenses. To do this he sold his family's land, restaurant, and wife's jewelry and borrowed from money lenders. Once in Scotland, he was imprisoned in the isolated hotel in a remote corner of the country. He worked 22 hours a day, seven days a week, and was not paid. He owned money to Arefin as well as the money lenders at home. He was threatened with deportation. He was physically abused. After a while, other Bangladeshis arrived and were enslaved. Everyone, including the local authorities, turned a blind eye. Finally, the hotel was raided. Abul was allowed to have a temporary work permit as long as he testified against Arefin. He took on temporary menial jobs, growing more destitute as the interest on his loans at home mounted. In 2015, Arefin was found guilty of human trafficking and imprisoned for three years. Meanwhile, Abul and the others have found jobs in Scotland that pay just enough to service their debts at home.[36]

Abul is a modern-day slave.

The experience of Abul is typical of traffickers exploiting an initial debt assumed by a worker as part of an employment contract. Men and women who migrate willingly to work in other countries end up in involuntary servitude with their documentation withheld and not being paid. High recruitment fees often result in debt bondage whereby the interest is more than the wages paid to the worker. The incentive for people seeking the promise of good-paying jobs and working conditions is the extreme poverty and high unemployment level of Bangladesh. Some women who take job offers through recruitment agencies to the

Middle East for domestic work are subsequently sold through traffickers to other countries and subjected to forced labor and sex trafficking. There are reports of forced labor in brick kiln factories and in shrimp farming. Reports also confirm that government officials are complicit in trafficking, and corruption among government officials and law enforcement is widespread.

In 2013 the Rana Plaza garment factory on the outskirts of Dhaka collapsed and 1,127 workers died. This brought international attention to the atrocious working conditions at the site. Pope Francis condemned the conditions of the workers who died in the factory as slave labor. "Living on 38 euros ($50) a month—that was the pay of these people who died. That is called slave labor," Francis said in a sermon.[37]

Bangladesh is located in South Asia bordering India and Myanmar and the Bay of Bengal. It was originally part of British India. In the 1947 partition of India it became part of Pakistan and was renamed East Pakistan in 1955. In 1971, it succeeded from Pakistan after a liberation war to become Bangladesh. While it is technically a secular multiparty parliamentary democracy, it has experienced instability with civil strife and military coups. Its gross domestic product is about the same as Vietnam, but a high population of about 161 million results in a per capita GDP among the lowest in the world.

There are 7.4 million child workers in Bangladesh between the ages of 5 and 17. Some children work on the streets picking up garbage, vending, and begging. Some begging children are maimed in order to enhance their appeal as beggars. Children are also involved in mining and manufacturing, including producing soap, matches, cigarettes, footwear, furniture, glass, leather, and textiles. Children in agriculture have to carry heavy loads, use dangerous tools, apply harmful pesticides, and work long hours in extreme temperatures. Children are also trafficked for domestic servitude and exploited in the commercial sex industry. There are an estimated 421,000 child domestic workers in the country who are shielded from scrutiny because they work behind closed doors.

However, there are reports of child abuse, threats, and sexual exploitation. According to Anti-Slavery International, there are nearly five million children between 5 and 15 working in hazardous conditions in factories, garages, and homes, in railway stations and markets, in small foundries, many for little or no pay.[38]

According to the Walk Free Foundation's 2016 Global Slavery Index there are 1,531,300 slaves in Bangladesh, representing 0.951 percent of the population. The country has the fourth largest number of slaves in its survey.

The US Department of State gives Bangladesh a Tier 2 ranking because the country is making an effort and is taking positive steps to reduce trafficking.

INDOCHINA

INDOCHINA REFERS TO THE AREA of Southeast Asia that is east of India and south of China consisting of the countries of Cambodia, Laos, Vietnam, Thailand, Myanmar, and Malaysia. With the exception of Thailand, these countries came under French and British colonial rule in the nineteenth century and gained their independence in the twentieth century. Depending on their proximity to India and China (hence the name Indochina), much of their historical culture reflects their much larger neighbor. All of these countries experience cross-border trafficking, illegal immigration, and kidnapping between and among themselves and their neighbors. They are sources, destinations, and transit countries for forced labor and sexual exploitation. Several of these countries also are affected by trafficking between India, China, Pakistan, and Bangladesh.

Thailand

THE KINGDOM OF THAILAND IS a hereditary constitutional monarchy that has been interrupted by military rule. A new constitution was passed by referendum in August 2016 to restore civilian rule. At this writing, the form of government is unknown. The economy is free enterprise-based with private property rights. Its Gross Domestic Product is about $400 billion, about the size of Austria.

The Guardian newspaper conducted a six-month investigation into the use of slaves in the shrimp fishing industry in Thailand, including interviews with dozens of boat captains, fishermen, boat managers, factory owners, government officials, and the victims of enslavement. Thailand is the world's largest shrimp exporter, a global trade estimated to exceed $7 billion annually. Increased demand for shrimp from the United States and Europe has made this a growth industry over the past decade. Thailand has a shortage of domestic labor for the fishing and shrimping sectors and the void is filled by migrant workers. Migrant workers from surrounding countries, primarily Burma and Cambodia, are lured to Thailand with the promise of good-paying jobs by brokers (traffickers). The "good-paying jobs" turn out to be servile jobs with no pay, little food, beatings, chains, and execution-style killings. The US Department of State estimates that there are two to three million migrant workers in Thailand, most of whom are from Burma. Corrupt government officials facilitate the smuggling of undocumented migrants between Thailand and neighboring countries.

The Walk Free Foundation estimates that there are 425,500 slaves in Thailand, many in the shrimping industry. *The Guardian*'s investigators found "a lawless and unregulated industry run by criminals and the Thai mafia—facilitated by Thai officials and sustained by the brokers who supply cheap migrant labour to boat owners."[39] *The Guardian* article states that, according to Thai officials, some 300,000 are employed in the fishing industry, 90 percent of whom are migrants.

Fishing vessels manned by slave labor use fishing nets to capture low-value fish in international waters. These fish are then sold to land-based factories that process the fish into fishmeal. The fishmeal is then used for feed for farmed prawns/shrimp. *The Guardian* report contained the following:

Men who have managed to escape from boats supplying CP Foods and other companies like it told *The Guardian* of horrific conditions, including 20-hour shifts, regular beatings, torture and execution-style killings. Some were at sea for years; some were regularly offered methamphetamines to keep them going. Some had seen fellow slaves murdered in front of them.

Fifteen migrant workers from Burma and Cambodia also told how they had been enslaved. They said they had paid brokers to help them find work in Thailand in factories or on building sites. But they had been sold instead to boat captains, sometimes for as little as £250....

Another trafficking victim said he had seen as many as 20 fellow slaves killed in front of him, one of whom was tied, limb by limb, to the bows of four boats and pulled apart at sea.

"We'd get beaten even if we worked hard," said another. "All the Burmese, [even] on all the other boats, were trafficked. There were so many of us [slaves] it would be impossible to count them all."[40]

These workers are modern-day slaves.

The US State Department 2016 on Trafficking in Persons Report ranks Thailand as a Tier 2 Watch List country, next to the lowest ranking in terms of conditions of slavery and slavery-like practices, but improved from the prior year's Tier 3 ranking. It estimates that there are thousands of persons, many of them immigrants, who are forced, coerced, or defrauded into forced labor or exploited in the sex trade. The leading usages for slave labor are the commercial fishing and fishing-related industries, the garment manufacturing industry, and domestic work. Victims include migrants from China, Vietnam, Russia, Uzbekistan, India, Fiji, as well as the contiguous countries Cambodia and Burma. The ranking is also a function of the government's lack of compliance with the minimum standards for the elimination of trafficking. Transparency and accountability are clouded by corruption, bribes, and payoffs involving local and federal law enforcement officials.

Cambodia

CAMBODIA LIES TO THE SOUTHEAST of Thailand, east of the Gulf of Thailand and to the west of Vietnam. It is a parliamentary constitutional monarchy that gained its independence from France in 1953. It is one of the poorest countries in the world with a Gross National Product of about $18 billion. The country is challenged with endemic corruption, limited human resources, high income inequality, poor educational opportunities, and poor job prospects, according to the *CIA World Fact Book*. About half of the country has been beset by political and civil strife, including the three-year rule of the Khmer Rouge under Pol Pot beginning in 1975, during which upwards of two million people died, and a ten-year occupation by Vietnam from 1978 to 1988. The country's transition to democratic governance is questioned.

The 2016 United States Trafficking in Persons Report states that all of Cambodia's provinces are sources of human trafficking. Because of the poor employment opportunities in Cambodia and the impoverished level of the population, adults and children migrate to other countries within the region and to the Middle East for work, only to be forced, coerced, or tricked into slave labor or sex work. They end up as slaves on fishing vessels, in agriculture, in construction, in factories, and in domestic help.

Svay Pak, a section of Cambodia's capital, Phnom Penh, is known for its child sex trafficking. About 75 percent of the victims of the sex trade are children. Some of the girls in the brothels are as young as 5. While some are tricked into prostitution, many are sold to the brothels by their parents in order to meet living expenses or to pay off debts. The brothel owners threaten the girls with violence if they try to escape or threaten harm to their family back home. The trade in virgins is also lucrative, with buyers willing to pay from $500 to $4,000 per girl. The low wages of law enforcement make the authorities vulnerable to bribes from brothel owners or voluntary prostitutes to look the other way.[41]

Chain Channi was a domestic worker in Malaysia from Cambodia who described her ordeal and work environment to Human Rights Watch:

> I woke up at 5 a.m., cleaned the house and made breakfast for the children and worked all day. I went to sleep at 3 a.m. I never got a chance to rest.... The wife of the employer shouted and beat me every day.... The employer had my passport. The door was locked. I was not allowed to go out or even talk to the neighbours. I never received my salary.[42]

The Walk Free Foundation 2016 Slavery Index estimates that there are 256,600 slaves in Cambodia, or about 1.65 percent of the 15.6 million population. Despite the third-highest percentage of the population in the world in slavery, the United States Department of State upgraded Cambodia to a Tier 2 Watch List ranking from Tier 3 because the country is making significant efforts to confront the problem.

Myanmar

MYANMAR, THE REPUBLIC OF THE Union of Myanmar, formerly Burma, is the most easterly country on the Southeastern Asia Peninsula. It borders the Bay of Bengal to the west and Bangladesh, India, China, Laos, and Thailand, going from west to east. A British colony in the nineteenth century, it gained its independence in 1948. A history of civil war among its many ethnic minorities and the Buddhist majority and economic mismanagement through the nationalization of all industries turned the country from one of the wealthiest in the region to one of the most impoverished. Following years of military dictatorship, a nominally civilian government was elected in 2010, and in 2015 free elections were held that promise a democratic future and economic reforms.

In 2016, the United States downgraded Myanmar to a ranking of Tier 3, the lowest ranking for a country in terms of human trafficking. The Walk Free Foundation's 2016 Slavery Index estimates that there are 515,100 enslaved within the country, representing 0.956 percent of a population total of just under 54 million. Because of the lack of employment opportunities in Myanmar and the impoverished condition of a large number of its people, it is a source for men, women, and children who are trafficked to neighboring countries through the use of fraud, coercion, trickery, and false promises for work and good-paying jobs. Women often end up in sexual exploitation conditions. According to the United States Department of State Trafficking in Person's Report, the government of Myanmar has not addressed the systemic political and economic problems that cause the people to seek employment through both legal and illegal means in neighboring countries.

The county's Rohingya Muslim minority, numbering over one million, are singled out for persecution by the Buddhist majority. Even though they have lived in Myanmar for generations, they are considered illegal immigrants and therefore have no standing as citizens. The police, military, and border control agencies engage in the unlawful conscription of Rohingya people from Rohingya villages.

Village authorities have to requisition quotas of unpaid workers on a daily basis according to the demands of the NaSaKa (the border security force) and the Army camps. There are also reports that roads, bridges, canals, and other public works are using forced labor in some instances with little or no remuneration. Forced labor for the NaSaKa and Army by individuals from Rohingya villages for maintenance, repair, cultivation, animal husbandry, portering, collection of forest products, and border sentry duty is widely reported. The use of children as young as 9 or 10 is pervasive.

The following quote from a 10-year-old Rohingya boy is representative of the forced labor that the Myanmar army and the NaSaKa imposes on these people:

I do forced labour sometimes 3 days, sometimes 5 days a month, in the NaSaKa camp. My father usually does the sentry duties, but sometimes I also have to do it when my father is sick. I try to stay awake during sentry duty because, whenever I fall asleep, my father has to give chickens. Because of forced labour I cannot go to school.[43]

This youth is a modern-day slave.

While the NaSaKa has subsequently been disbanded, its activities have been taken over by the Myanmar Border Police, and human rights violations continue.[44]

An October 28, 2014, article in the *Wall Street Journal* entitled "Human Traffickers in Bay of Bengal Cast Sights on Bangladesh" tells of criminal gangs from Myanmar going to Bangladesh to recruit people with the promise of good-paying jobs in Malaysia or other neighboring countries. The gangs also kidnap people and sell them to traffickers or employers who enslave them, mostly to work on fishing vessels. Abul Hasan was a 30-year-old fisherman living in Bangladesh when he was approached by a trafficker who promised him a good-paying job in Malaysia. He was given a drugged drink and, upon awakening, found himself with other victims on a boat in the bay. He was going to be sold into slavery. Fortunately, the police raided the boat and he was freed. Others were not so lucky.[45]

A United Nations report stated that the Rohingya are subject to a web of abuse by state security officials including summary executions, enforced disappearances, arbitrary arrests and detention, torture and ill-treatment, and forced labor.[46]

CHINA

KIAB GREW UP IN VIETNAM with her family. When Kiab turned 16, her brother promised to take her to a party in a tourist town in northern Vietnam. Instead, he sold her to a trafficker who sold her to a Chinese family as a bride.

"My brother is no longer a human being in my eyes—he sold his own sister to China....

"I had heard a lot about trafficking. But I couldn't imagine it would happen to me," Kiab said.[47]

Kiab is a modern-day slave.

The People's Republic of China, located in East Asia, is the world's most populous country, with about 1.35 billion people. Following WWII and a civil war, the Communist Party established the People's Republic in 1949. It is a single-political-party socialist government. As such, much of the means of production and distribution are owned by the state. Although there have been steps toward economic and political liberalization in recent years, the Communist Party controls elections, the press, and freedom of expression, and human rights are compromised. China's gross domestic product ranks second in the world at approximately $8.2 trillion.

In countries that border China, girls are sold as brides for forced marriages or to brothels. China's one-child policy and a preference for a male child have resulted in the abortion of females and a resulting gender imbalance. Millions of Chinese men cannot find female Chinese brides and therefore turn to traffickers to buy their wives. Chinese men who propose marriage to a Chinese woman often are expected to pay for an expensive wedding and have a home in which to live. Foreign brides are much less expensive.

Lan was preparing for college and lived in a town in Vietnam that bordered China. A friend invited her to a party where she was drugged, smuggled across the border to China by a trafficker and sold to a Chinese man and forced into marriage.

"When I woke up I didn't know that I was in China....

"At that time, I wanted to leave. There were other girls there in the car but there was people to guard us."[48]

Lan is a modern-day slave.

Harry Wu was a survivor of the forced labor camps of China.

> "At that time, most of the prisoners took advantage of labor-
> ing in the fields to bring back a variety of roots, wild herbs,
> and bones. Then they would fill a wash basin with water and
> boil and eat them. People were looking for anything that could
> stave off hunger and provide energy."[49]

Harry was a modern-day slave.

Harry Wu went on to head the Laogai Research Foundation in Washington, DC, a nonprofit humanitarian group. Beginning as a teenager, Wu spent 19 years in 12 different camps before being released in 1979. Wu was arrested in 1960 without explanation or legal or judicial proceedings. In 1985 Wu came to the United States and joined the faculty of the University of California, Berkeley. While entering China in 1995, he was accused of stealing state secrets and sentenced to 15 years' imprisonment. Because of an international uproar, Wu was freed from China. Wu was nominated for the Nobel Peace Prize for his work in exposing the forced labor camps of China and the products made from slave labor that enter the world economy. The Laogai Foundation has exposed more than 1,000 forced labor camps in China that are currently active. The word *laogai* means "reform through labor" and the camps are an outgrowth of the Great Leap Forward and the Cultural Revolution. The camps are home to common criminals as well as those deemed to be political enemies of the government. The inhabitants are incarcerated for statutory crimes and arbitrary, vague, and often made-up charges of having done something not in the national interest; as such, they are labeled "ideological reactionaries." Often the internment period has no terminal date. Wu related his narrative in the book *Enslaved*. His most vivid memories of his early years of internment were of death and hunger.

Mr. Li Yaokai, an 18-year-old from central China, was kidnapped from a train station and sold into slavery at a brick factory. For three months, he labored in the brick factory 17 hours a day, with no pay. He was fed a subsistence level diet of bread, noodles, and water. He was beaten when he became too weak or exhausted to do the work. He was surrounded and guarded by watchdogs and men carrying iron bars as weapons. People, mostly young men, are either abducted or lured to places of hire with the promise of well-paying jobs. They are then sold to factories or mines and held in bondage, performing hard work with no pay and in deplorable conditions. The forced labor factories and mines are often in collaboration with local authorities, who receive bribes from the labor camp owners. Mr. Li was freed from the camp along with other workers when police raided the brick factory. Millions of Chinese have left their villages to seek work. These migrant workers are easy prey to the slave traffickers and, given the size of the country and widespread illiteracy, the families of the missing may not realize that the victims have been abducted or kidnapped. A groundswell of concern eventually leads to police raids on some of the factories and, in this case, the release of Mr. Li.[50]

> China is still freeing people enslaved in illegal brick factories, officials said, two months after Chinese media reported that children as young as 8 years old were abducted and sold to kilns for about 500 yuan ($66). "Another 359 slave migrant workers have been rescued in Shanxi since late June, including 15 child workers and 121 mentally handicapped ones," Xue Yanzhong, executive vice-governor of Shanxi province, said in a statement on the central government's website. The workers were found in 17 brick kilns, he said. A labor official said 147 suspects who ran the kilns had been arrested.[51]

Forced labor remains a serious problem in China. Workers, some as young as 8, are abducted, kidnapped, or coerced into enslaved forced labor. They endure little or no shelter, are poorly clothed, and given subsistence level food and water. They receive no pay. Many of the brick

117

kiln factories where these enslaved workers toil are in remote and isolated areas, and local officials are bribed by the factory owners. There were reports that local officials aided the owners of closed factories in selling the workers to other brick kiln owners.

The report also confirmed that many Chinese men are promised well-paid jobs by recruiters and traffickers, in other countries including Mexico, Japan, Australia, the Netherlands, and Argentina, only to find themselves forced into slavery.[52]

The Walk Free Foundation's 2016 Global Slavery Index estimates that there are 3.4 million persons enslaved in China, representing 0.247 of the population.

The 2016 US Department of State Trafficking in Persons Report states that Chinese men, women, and children are subjected to forced labor in brick kilns, coal mines, and factories. The internal migrant population is estimated to exceed 236 million and trafficking is reportedly widespread among this group. State-sponsored forced labor camps are a problem of significant concern. The report states that there are at least 320 forced labor camps controlled by the government. Criminal syndicates and local gangs are also involved in sex trafficking of women and girls from rural areas to urban areas.

Chinese men, women, and children from within China are subjected to forced labor and sex trafficking in other countries. This is particularly true in overseas Chinese communities. They are forced to work as laborers and in the service sector, in restaurants and as domestic help. Chinese men are trafficked abroad to work at construction sites and in coal and copper mines in Africa. Their passports are withheld, they are subjected to physical abuse, confinement to the workplace, and the non-payment of wages. Through the threat of violence and beatings, women and girls are forced into prostitution in urban brothels, at construction sites, and logging and mining camps.

Foreigners are also abducted, kidnapped, or coerced into working within China in conditions of slavery. Employers confiscate documents if they exist and provide subsistence level food, deplorable shelter facilities and do not pay wages. Illiteracy and inability to speak the local language increase the victims' vulnerability to the employer. Local officials are also corrupted through bribes from the employers.

China is ranked as a Tier 2 Watch List country meaning that the country could be downgraded to Tier 3 if it does not take additional steps to address trafficking. In 2013 the country, was ranked as a Tier 3 country. Thus, the State Department in its 2016 report did recognize some progress in meeting the minimum standards for anti-trafficking law enforcement.

UZBEKISTAN

Sukhrob Ismoilov began picking cotton when he was eleven years old. He was forced to pick cotton by the government and fulfill a daily quota, working eleven to twelve hours a day during the harvest season that ran from August to October. He slept in barracks and was not permitted to attend school during the harvest season. If he became injured or ill, he did not have access to adequate healthcare. "People miss their homes, their work. The food is poor, the sanitation is poor. It is servitude."[53]

Uzbekistan is a socialist/authoritarian landlocked country in Central Asia. It became part of the Russian Empire in the nineteenth century and the Soviet Union in 1924. With the collapse of the Soviet Union in 1991, it became an independent country. Uzbekistan has a gross domestic product of about $52 billion, or about the same size as Guatemala. The economy is tightly controlled by the government and is highly dependent on agriculture and natural resources. It is one of the world's largest cotton producers. About 25 percent of the country's gross domestic product is connected to the cotton sector. Farmers are ordered by the government to grow cotton and fulfill production quotas. The government requisitions workers from both the public sector and the private sectors to weed the cotton fields in the spring and harvest the cotton in the fall. Workers from the public sector who are forced into this work include teachers, doctors, nurses, and administers, and as a result, these sectors of the economy are underserved and contribute to the underperformance of the country in general. Private companies that do not mobilize workers for labor in the fields are subject to fines or increased taxes. Students are also forced to work during the seasonal periods. The government openly confronts, harasses, and detains human rights observers to prevent them from reporting the trafficking that takes place.

In addition to forced labor in the agricultural sector, the United States Department of State Trafficking in Persons Report states that the country is a source and destination for men, women, and children in other areas of forced labor, including construction, oil, and food service. Women and children are subject to sex trafficking both within the country and outside the country.

Uzbekistan distinguishes itself by having the fifth-highest absolute number of slaves in the world and the second highest prevalence of slavery, according to the Walk Free Foundation's Global Slavery Index. In the 2016 report Uzbekistan had 1,236,600 people enslaved representing 3.97 percent of its population of about 31 million. The US Department of State ranks the country Tier 3, the lowest ranking for confronting modern-day slavery.

RUSSIA

LEYLA ASHEROVA WAS 16 WHEN she was kidnapped from Uzbekistan, trafficked to Russia and enslaved in a Moscow mini-market. She had worked in the store for ten years and had two children born into captivity. The father of her children was a member of the shop owner's family. The store had eleven slaves. Another five-year-old boy working in the shop had been locked inside his entire life, he had never seen daylight. The shop owners bribed the local authorities.

She said the hours worked in the mini-market were long, the food was meagre and she lived in constant fear of violence.

"The shop owner beat me a lot," she explained. "Once she beat me non-stop for two hours. I still have bruises on my legs, on my body, and on my face. She even hit me when I was pregnant...."

"Even when they [other girls] asked the police for help, they didn't get any. The policemen would simply bring them back to the owner. They would arrive and say, 'We've got your girls. Take them back.' So we couldn't trust the police. We were scared to run away because we thought we'd be found and beaten."[54]

Leyla is a modern-day slave.

Leyla and the others were rescued by Alternative, an anti-slavery labor organization headquartered in Moscow, with offices around the country. After Leyla was freed, she was arrested by the local police for illegal immigration because the shop owner had confiscated and presumably destroyed her passport. Once Leyla was freed again by Alternative, the federal and local authorities failed to prosecute the perpetrators, and the case was closed.

oDR: Russia and Beyond is a Russian multimedia/language news organization that investigates human rights abuses in Russia, as well as other topical subjects of interest. It also published an article on the mini-store slaves entitled "Russia, Land of Slaves."

In a special oDR: Russia and Beyond investigation, reporter Grigory Tumanov comments on the worrying prevalence of modern-day enslavement within Russia. The reporter relates how army conscripts are hired out to local contractors, receive no pay, food, or medical help and live in confinement. The officers receive remuneration from the contractors. Women from within Russia from the most disadvantaged social groups are seduced and coerced into taking a job, either in Russia or another country such as Turkey, only to find themselves sold to a brothel. Their documents are taken, and they are threatened with violence if they try to escape. Other slave exploits detailed in the article include women and children forced into begging for their masters. The local police are not interested in prosecuting the enslavers or traffickers because the victims are held in such low esteem: migrants, foreigners, homeless, mentally handicapped, and prostitutes. The authorities themselves are often corrupt and accept bribes.

> It is impossible to actually calculate how many slaves there are in Russia today. In the police department responsible for investigating cases of illegal imprisonment and kidnappings, they tell me that all the instances mentioned in this article come under different articles of the Criminal Code, so it is not possible to come up with an overall figure.

> "Russian law doesn't recognise the concept of slavery," they say, shrugging their shoulders, "so we have no way of calculating the number of slaves in Russia. And as far as kidnappings are concerned, the figures may even be going down, but the figures don't distinguish between kidnappings for ransom and kidnappings into slavery."[55]

An article by Allison Quinn entitled "How to Free a Modern-Day Slave in Dagestan" was published in the *Moscow Times*. Dagestan is one of the republics within The Russia Federation, with its capital Makhachkala on the Caspian Sea. The article tells the stories of enslaved persons in brick factories in Makhachkala. The stories follow a familiar refrain. The factory owners hire traffickers to recruit vulnerable and gullible people in Moscow with offers of well-paying jobs. They often offer the recruit a laced drink and then transport them to Makhachkala to work in the factories. Life in the factories is not what was promised.

One story is that of Vadim Pushkin. "There is an organized group that recruits these people in Moscow and transports them back here," said Zakir Ismailov, a worker for the human rights group Alternative.

> He [Pushkin] wound up at the factory after falling for promises of decent work and a good salary while at a Moscow train station, where such forced labor scams often begin.

> They usually involve trickery and promises of solid employment, Ismailov says, or, in the worst case scenario, a cup of tea laced with a tranquilizer. The recruiters find someone who seems to be down on their luck, strike up a conversation and feign empathy, then offer a cup of tea or a shot of vodka to drown their sorrows. After that, they put him on a bus to Makhachkala, where he will be met by modern-day slave traders upon arrival....

> According to Ismailov, corruption is a complicating factor in prosecuting the factory owners, especially since most of them have relatives working in law enforcement....

> Prosecution is also impeded by the victims' reluctance to stick around for legal proceedings....

> At the same time, many of the victims stay [enslaved] not because they are chained up or physically detained, but because they are so terrified of leaving. "They detain them morally, psychologically, not physically. They break them," Ismailov said.[56]

Vadim is a modern-day slave.

Russia is the largest country in the world in terms of land mass. Officially named the Russian Federation, it emerged from the dissolution of the Soviet Union in 1991. Russia is considered a federal, semi-presidential republic, although its president has semi-dictatorial power. Its economy is the twelfth largest in the world in terms of nominal gross domestic product and the sixth largest in terms of purchasing power parity.

The English language newsletter *Russia Beyond the Headlines* published a report entitled "Russia's Hidden Slave Labor Market." According to the article, there are between 490,000 and 1 million people entrapped in slave-like conditions in Russia. A common kidnapping occurrence, as we have seen, is for a trafficker to offer a drink laced with a powerful drug to a person at a bus or train station. The person ends up being transported to a factory where he is sold to the employer. They work long hours, seven days a week, are sometimes beaten, and live in confined conditions, often several to a trailer. A trafficker receives on average $500 for the sale of a male slave. The trafficker may have paid as little as one-fifth that for the victim.

The article recites the work of Alternative, the anti-slave labor NGO in Moscow, that has freed more than 120 slaves. The authorities are of little help to those enslaved.

> Alternative members saved Alleg Fetkhulov. He came to Moscow to work and was approached by two Caucasians at the station offering him a drink.

> Alleg came to, like the rest of the kidnapped people, in a bus already in Dagestan. Alleg was sent to a factory where the slaves were not beaten, were well fed, and were even given cigarettes. They lived five to a trailer and worked from 6 a.m. to 9 p.m., seven days a week.

> Alleg's wife Olga called the authorities. First she went to the Federal Security Service, then to the police, but only the activists of Alternative could help her release Alleg.[57]

While Alleg was well-treated, he was not free. He is a modern-day slave.

Russian and former Soviet Bloc countries' newspapers and magazines carry ads for well-paying jobs directed at young women. The women are lured by ads because of the high unemployment rate in their area, their own poverty, and naivety. The ads proclaim "great jobs, have your own apartment, earn lots of money." Instead, the girls end up as sex slaves.

A BBC report disclosed a factory run by Vietnamese outside of Moscow where some 75 Vietnamese had been enslaved, working 18 hours a day, seven days a week. They were poorly fed, confined to the factory grounds, and beaten regularly. They shared four small rooms that had no electricity and insufficient water with which to bathe. Electricity plugs were removed from the rooms and work areas so they could not charge their cells phones. Their passports and other documentation were taken from them. They were lured to the factory with the promise of high-paying jobs and guaranteed employment. They paid a recruiter as an employment agency and owed that debt plus had to pay the employer for their food and housing. Their actual pay was less than what they owed and with interest charges the workers' debts accumulated with each passing month. They became debtor slaves. Police investigating the factory decided to not bring criminal charges against the owners of the factory. BBC reported that this factory was just one of dozens of similar factories run by Vietnamese entrepreneurs in Russia.[58]

These workers are modern-day slaves.

The Walk Free Foundation ranks Russia seventh in the world in terms of the absolute number of slaves within its borders. They project that there are 1.048 million enslaved in Russia, mostly immigrants doing forced work in agricultural, construction, manufacturing, grocery store, maritime, textile, garment, and domestic service industries. Russia has a total population of 143.3 million. The US Department of State in its 2016 Trafficking in Persons Report states that Russia is a source, transit, and destination country for men, women, and children subject to forced labor and sex trafficking. It is estimated that there are between five and twelve million foreign workers in Russia. Their areas of origin include Europe, Central Asia, and Southeast Asia. These immigrant workers are especially vulnerable to traffickers who take advantage of their poverty, illiteracy, and inability to speak the local language. Once they are sold by the trafficker to a dealer and the dealer sells them to an employer, the immigrants' passports and other documents are confiscated and they are subjected to forced labor, malnutrition, lack of medical care, beatings and often death.

The US Department of State and Human Rights Watch both report that forced labor and slavery and slavery-like conditions are widespread within Russia. They confirm that Russian authorities are complicit in the non-enforcement of laws against trafficking and that corruption is evident at local and national levels. According to the US Department of State 2016 Trafficking in Persons report, "The Government of Russia does not fully comply with the minimum standards for the elimination of trafficking and is not making significant efforts to do so." The report gives Russia a Tier 3 ranking.

CHAPTER SIX

The New World

TODAY VIRTUALLY EVERY COUNTRY IN North and South America experiences forced and involuntary servitude and sex trafficking, according to the United States Department of State's Trafficking in Persons Report, the Walk Free Foundation, and other non-profit humanitarian organizations. Many of these counties participated in the Atlantic slave trade and, indeed, most of their native indigenous populations experienced slavery before the arrival of the Europeans.

The Caribbean Islands

CHRISTOPHER COLUMBUS SET SAIL FROM Palos, Spain, with eighty-eight men on August 3, 1492, in hopes of finding a westward passage to India or "The Indies." The impetus for Spain to find a westward passage to the Orient was born out of the conflicts between the Christians and the Muslims. The Crusades had failed to open up the land and sea trade routes from Europe to Asia. The Islamic Ottoman Empire controlled the eastern Mediterranean, as well as large parts of Eastern Europe, the Middle East, and Asia Minor. In 1453, Constantinople (Istanbul) fell to the Muslims. Constantinople was a major trade route between Europe and Asia. The Eastern Roman Empire (the Byzantine Empire) that had protected Europe from Asia for a thousand years, was now in the hands of the Turks. As a result, trade routes to India, China, and the Orient were closed, dangerous to traverse, or costly because of high tariffs to Europeans. As the most westerly of the European countries, Portugal and Spain, felt compelled to find a westerly passage to Asia across the ocean.

An additional motive to finding a direct route to the Indies was to exploit the "riches" that were thought to be there. Ever since Marco Polo had returned from his twenty-four-year adventure to the Orient in the early fourteenth century with tales of stupendous wealth, Europeans dreamed of a westward passage to the Far East. The land that was spotted on October 14, 1492 was one of the islands of the Bahamas known as San Salvador or Watling Island and called Guanahani by the local tribes.

On shore, Columbus met the Taino tribe, a part of a larger linguistic group known as the Arawaks. The Taino were primitive by European standards but were generally peaceful until mistreated by the Spanish, and slavery does not appear to have been widely practiced. After establishing a fort on Hispaniola, today home to Haiti and the Dominican Republic, Columbus returned to Spain. The fort was named La Navidad and was the first recorded settlement by Europeans in the New World.

To the south of Hispaniola, Columbus also encountered another American Indian tribe, the Caribs. The Caribs were a fierce warrior tribe that intimidated the more peaceful and sedentary Taino. They had the reputation of being cannibals, a continuation of the practice of their forebears in South America. The Caribs raided Taino settlements, driving them northward, killing the male captives and eating them while taking the women and children as slaves. Women and girl captives were used to produce babies that the Caribs ate as well. Columbus mentions the Caribs in his letter to the Crown:

> We asked the women who were held prisoners on this island what kind of people these were; and they replied that they were Caribs. When they understood that we hated these people on account of their cannibalism, they were highly delighted. They do not harm each other but all make war against the neighbouring islands. These people raid the other islands and carry off all the women they can take, especially the young and

beautiful, whom they keep as servants and concubines. These women say that they are treated with cruelty that seems incredible. The Caribs eat the male children that they have by them, and only bring up the children of their own women; and as for the men they are able to capture, they bring those who are alive home to be slaughtered and eat those who are dead on the spot. They castrate the boys that they capture and use them as servants until they are men. Then, when they want to make a feast, they kill and eat them.[1]

Slavery was alive and well in the New World as well as the Old!

On Columbus's return to Europe, he brought seven to ten captive Taino Indians. Thus, the first recorded slaves to cross the Atlantic went from west—the New World—to east—the Old World. Bad weather resulted in Columbus landing in Lisbon, Portugal. Since Portugal and Spain were adversaries, Columbus had to do some fast talking.

And as undeniable evidence that he had been to an undiscovered country, Columbus selected some of the healthiest specimens of his ten captive Indians to share the royal weekend. After being subjected to the terrors of the deep, these poor creatures were now to experience the horrors of mule back navigation in Portugal; unless, as is likely, they were required to trudge barefoot in the mud. And to be stroked and pinched by the curious crowds in the street of Lisbon. A "great pestilence" was then raging along the lower Tagus, but Nina's company, both white and red, fortunately escaped contamination.[2]

The intentions of Columbus regarding commerce in slaves are unknown, since his main goal was finding a passage to India. This having not been successful, his attention turned to finding gold, planting the Spanish flag, and Christianizing the natives.

But once Columbus encountered the Taino, he realized that they might indeed be useful as slaves.

There never crossed the mind of Columbus, or his fellow discoverers and conquistadors, any other notion of relations between Spaniard and American Indian save that of master and slave. It was a conception founded on the Spanish enslavement of Guanches in the Canaries, and on the Portuguese enslavement of Negroes in Africa, which Columbus had observed and taken for granted, and which the Church condoned.[3]

However, should your Highness command it all the inhabitants could be taken away to Castile or held as slaves on the island, for with fifty men we could subjugate them all and make them do whatever we wish.[4]

Here there is a vast quantity of gold, and from here and other islands I bring Indians as evidence. In conclusion, to speak only of the results of this very hasty voyage, their Highnesses can see that I will give them as much gold as they require, if they will render me some very slight assistance; also I will give them all the spices and cotton they want, and as for mastic, which has so far been found only in Greece and the island of Chios and which the Genoese authorities have sold at their own price, I will bring back as large a cargo as their Highnesses may command. I will also bring them as much aloes as they ask and as many slaves, who will be taken from the idolaters.[5]

On subsequent voyages, the Spaniards shipped the inhabitants of the Caribbean Islands back to Iberia to be sold on the slave markets of Europe. The American Indians by now were rebelling against the Spanish, who in turn embarked on "pacification" expeditions, killing, raping, and enslaving the natives. Hispaniola is thought to have contained about 300,000 natives at the time of Columbus's first landing. A census of 1508 recorded 60,000 Indians and they declined to the point of extinction after that.[6]

Oppressive labor, disruption of the Indian food supply, deliberate campaigns of extermination, and especially disease decimated the Indian population. Isolated from such diseases as smallpox, influenza, and measles, the indigenous population proved to be extraordinarily susceptible. Within a century of contact, the Indian population in the Caribbean and Mexico had shrunk by more than 90 percent.[7]

The rapid decline in the native population and the campaign by human rights activist Bartolome de las Casas (1484–1566) for better treatment of the natives led to the importation of African slaves as the main source of labor for the islands of the Caribbean and in time the plantations of North and South America.

Haiti

HAITI IS A COUNTRY ON THE western three-eighths of the island of Hispaniola. Haiti has a population of about eleven million, half of whom live on less than one dollar a day, and 80 percent of the population live below the poverty rate. It has a literacy rate of just 53 percent. The high poverty rate and lack of infrastructure and basic services result in impoverished families being vulnerable as victims to forced labor and sexual exploitation.

Marie Alina "Tibebe" Cajuste was a victim of Haiti's restavek system, whereby families send their children, through a trafficker, to live with other families in distant cities in the hope that the young girls and boys would be afforded an opportunity to escape the impoverished condition of their own family in return for domestic help. Instead, the children end up in homes where they are subjected to sexual exploitation, abuse, neglect, beatings, and confinement. They are not paid for their work and are at the mercy of their master. When Tibebe's mother became pregnant, she was thrown out of the house.

"I was born on the street in front of a brothel. Prostitutes brought my mother a towel, so she could swaddle me. My father's mistress was beautiful, and she, too, had a daughter that day, but she died on that day. My father gave me my sister's name."[8]

Tibebe's mother is a modern-day slave.

Jean-Robert Cadet was sent to another family at age 4. He swept the yard, washed the car, cleaned the bathroom, emptied the chamber pot, and was physically abused and beaten with a whip. He lost all contact with his natural family, thereby experiencing natal alienation.

"It never occurred to me that I was treated wrong, because I started at such a young age.... And as a child, to me, the children who didn't have mothers and fathers were restaveks and the children who had mothers and fathers were normal children. So I knew I was not normal, there was something wrong with me as a child, there was something that I lacked that caused me to be in the situation that I was in."

In an interview Cadet explained his sense of isolation and the whip that was used:

"In the society as a whole they [restavek children] are invisible because they are confined in the backyard. They are invisible because they cannot go to schools, they are invisible because they are not seen as a regular member of society....

It's the same whip that the French used during colonial times to beat slaves."[9]

Cadet is a modern-day slave.

Most of Haiti's trafficking victims, estimated to total between 200,00 and 300,000, are children who are subjected to the restavek system. They do not have birth certificates and are not registered with the government. They do not attend school. Despite the abuses of the restavek system, impoverished families continue to send their children through traffickers to wealthier families in the hope that they will be better off, as well as to relieve their burden of raising a child. In many cases, these wealthier families are also below the poverty level, but they need domestic workers to do house labor. A significant number of children flee the homes they are sent to because of abusive treatment and end up becoming street children or prostitutes.[10]

Haiti's history of slavery dates to its initial colonization by the Spanish. The island of Hispaniola was divided between Spain and France in 1697, with the eastern portion going to the Spanish and eventually becoming the Dominican Republic, and the western portion ceded to the French.

Haiti, originally named Saint Domingue by the French, was sparsely populated when it was ceded to the French. The economy was supported by tanning hides and tobacco and indigo production. There was less than a handful of sugar production. Overseas absentee landowners began to invest in sugar and the number of sugar plantations rose from 18 in 1700 to 793 in 1791, when the slave rebellion broke out. At that time Haiti was the largest sugar producing (and therefore wealth producing) colony in the Caribbean and perhaps the world.

The labor for the sugar plantations on Haiti was African slaves. The slave population of Haiti rose from around 3,000 in 1687 to about 465,400 in 1789. In the 1780s about 32,000 slaves were imported each year to Haiti. Sugar planting, harvesting, and milling was grueling and dangerous work in a tropical environment. The slaves were susceptible to disease, malnutrition, and mistreatment. There was a high death rate, resulting in the constant need for replenishment of workers. Additionally, the laws that governed slavery allowed the owners to manumit slaves.[11]

A growing portion of the population was free coloreds, the offspring of white fathers and African mothers. At the time of the slave revolution in 1789, free coloreds totaled 28,000, almost equal to the white population of 30,000. The free coloreds could own property, including plantations, and many owned slaves. The slave population, however, outnumbered the white population 15 to 1.

In 1789 a massive slave insurrection broke out. The revolt was led by Toussaint Louverture, a free black African. Before the revolution was over in 1803, a chaotic war raged in Haiti involving the French, the Spanish, and the British, and the indigenous whites, free coloreds, and blacks. The former slaves won and declared the colony independent on January 1, 1804. The Haitian Revolution was the largest and most successful slave revolt in history and Haiti was the second independent republic in the new world.

Haiti's history since its independence has been one of instability involving dictators, kings, foreign invasion and occupation by nations including the United States, and of limited periods of democratic rule.

The estimated number of modern-day slaves in Haiti today vary widely. The Walk Free Foundation's 2016 report estimates that there are 106,000 enslaved people within Haiti, less than half the number they estimated in their 2014 survey. This represents 0.995 percent of the population of 10.7 million, placing Haiti tied for 8th in the world in terms of the proportion of the population enslaved. Other non-profit organizations estimate the slavery population of Haiti today to range between 200,000 to 300,000.[12]

The US Department of State gives Haiti a Tier 3 ranking in that the government does not meet the minimum standards for the elimination of trafficking and did not demonstrate overall increasing efforts compared to the previous reporting period. The department also noted that Haiti is a source, transit, and destination country for men, women, and children subjected to forced labor and sex trafficking.

Dominican Republic

A 10-YEAR-OLD BOY from Haiti had been kidnapped near the Dominican border and taken to a camp for sugarcane workers in the Dominican Republic. He has been working for two months, has had no contact with his Haitian family, and is housed with other Haitians of similar fate, working as a slave.

"Can't you see how black my hands are? Nobody knows I'm here."[13]

This boy is a modern-day slave.

The Dominican Republic occupies the eastern five-eighths of the island of Hispaniola. It was settled by the Spanish and ultimately gained its independence from Haitian rule in 1844. The first black African slaves were brought to the island in 1502–1503. For further information on the discovery of the island by Columbus, see the section on Haiti. After years of internal strife, civil war, military dictatorship, and foreign intervention, the country is now a representative democracy. Initially the country's economy was dependent on farming, including sugar, coffee, tobacco, and on ranching and livestock. Although the Dominican Republic did not develop the large sugar plantations of Haiti, sugar is still an important part of the agricultural economy. Since sugar was a smaller part of the economy, fewer black African slaves were imported. The country has transitioned away from agriculture and is now the largest economy in the Caribbean and Central American region. Despite its vibrant economy led by manufacturing, telecommunications, and tourism, it is plagued by income inequality, government corruption, and large migrant flows that are conducive to forced and involuntary labor and sexual exploitation. Seventy-three percent of the population is multiracial, 16 percent is white, and 11 percent is black.

It is estimated that some 650,000–1,000,000 Haitians work in the sugarcane plantations in the Dominican Republic. The Dominican Republic has a higher standard of living than Haiti, and many Dominicans refuse to work in the slave-like conditions of the sugar plantations. Thus recruiters and traffickers kidnap, coerce, or fraudulently induce Haitians to work in the sugar fields of the Dominican Republic. The payment of bribes to local law enforcement allows this practice to continue. Given the high unemployment in Haiti, many are eager to seek work, only to find in many cases that they are treated as slaves, working 12-hour days, seven days a week, under armed guard for as little as $1 to $2 a day. Instead of cash, some are paid in vouchers that can only be redeemed for overpriced food at company-owned stores. They stay in barracks and dorms that they must pay for and which lack electricity and running water. Often they have to borrow money from the employer that they can't pay back and thus become bonded labor. The children born on the workplace are stateless, lacking either Haitian and Dominican citizenship and nationality. Dominicans generally are highly prejudiced and discriminate against Haitians, believing them to be lower class.[14]

The United States Department of State notes that sex trafficking and forced labor are also prevalent in the construction and services industries. Large numbers of women and children in the Dominican Republic are subjected to sex trafficking both within the country and in destinations throughout the world. Commercial sexual exploitation of local children by foreign tourists and locals persists, particularly in coastal resort areas, and foreign women brought to the country by traffickers are forced into prostitution.

The Global Slavery Index of 2016 estimates that there are 104,800 slaves in the country, representing 0.995 percent of the population of 10.5 million. This estimate is well below the estimates of others cited earlier. The country is given a Tier 2 ranking in that it is not fully complying with the minimum standards for the elimination of trafficking. According to the Index, Haiti and the Dominican Republic have the highest percentage of their population in slavery of any Western Hemisphere country.

CENTRAL and SOUTH AMERICA

Mexico

PEDRO BECAME A SEX TRAFFICKER at age 19. He came from an area in the state of Tlaxcala in central Mexico that was known for producing pimps. He started by offering candy to a young girl from an impoverished family. Within a week he proposed to marry her but stated he had to pay off a debt that in fact did not exist. By now she was mentally enslaved, seeing Pedro as a way to escape her condition of poverty. She agreed to have sex with clients to help Pedro pay off his debt before getting married. She entered a life of prostitution which for nine years she never left. She was never paid for any of her earnings. Some years later Pedro was later arrested and went to prison. Pedro recounted his experience in an interview:

> I never had any problem activating my girls. I knew lots of pimps who drugged and beat their women all the time. I knew pimps who kept them near starved and kept their children hostage, but it wasn't the school I was taught in.[15]

Pedro's girls are modern-day slaves.

Mexico has the largest number of slaves in the Americas, totaling 376,800 according to the Walk Free Foundation's 2016 Global Slavery Index. However, this only represents 0.297 percent of its population of about 127 million. About 70 percent of modern-day slavery in Mexico is related to the criminal cartels that often operate with the complicity of local law enforcement. These groups kidnap women and girls and sell them to work as domestic help and prostitutes.[16]

Following Mexico's war of independence with Spain in 1821, and after another two-year war that ended in 1848, Mexico ceded one-third of its territory to the United States. This was followed by political instability, civil war, dictatorships, and foreign interventions. The constitution of 1917 established the current political system of a federal presidential constitutional republic through democratic elections. It has recently undertaken to privatize several state-owned companies. The economy is the 14th largest in the world in nominal gross domestic product and in terms of purchasing power parity the 11th largest. Its economy is approximately the same size as that of South Korea and Spain.

Mexico is a largely agricultural economy, and although it accounts for less than 4 percent of gross domestic product, about 15 percent of the workforce is involved in growing crops and raising livestock. There are reports of slave-like conditions for some of the workers. Many farm workers have their wages withheld so that they will not leave during the working season. Many are housed in camps with barbed wire fences and armed guards, without beds, toilets, or reliable water supply. Workers are restricted to buying necessities at company stores at inflated prices, causing them to borrow money from the employers, creating debtor slaves. They are often threatened with violence or actual beatings if they are deemed out of line.[17]

Mexico has a long history of slavery dating to before 1519, the year that Cortes sailed from Cuba to invade the Aztec Empire. Slavery was practiced by the native tribes that the Spanish had encountered in the New World. The Spanish Crown had already established rules and orders regarding the indigenous people. Initially the Spaniards were to enslave only the natives who did not accept Christianity, as mandated by Pope Alexander VI in 1493. In 1500, Queen Isabella mandated that all Indians were to be free of slavery, but as has happened in all of history, what is required by law is not always followed in practice. As the indigenous population of Mexico were enslaved by the Spanish, many died from European diseases as well as mistreatment. The Spanish then turned to Africa for its supply of workers for the mines and the fields. The first black African to enter Mexico was probably an attendant of Cortes. He came from Spain and may or may not have been a slave. King Charles V of Spain (1500–1558) issued decrees that opened up the Atlantic slave trade to Mexico. Over the course of the next 300 years, about 200,000 black African slaves were imported to Mexico. In 1570, the black population of Mexico was about three times the Spanish population, and it was not until 1810 that the Spanish population outnumbered blacks. Mexico outlawed slavery in 1823.[18]

The United States Department of State Trafficking in Persons Report for 2016 states that Mexico is a source, transit, and destination country for men, women, and children subjected to sex trafficking and forced labor. Forced labor occurs in agriculture, domestic service, manufacturing, food processing, construction, forced begging, the informal economy, and street vending. The victims are lured by fraudulent labor recruiters, deceptive offers of romantic relationships, or extortion. Often times identity papers and documents are confiscated, and the perpetrators will threaten harm to the victims' families, the vast majority of whom come from Central and South America. Organized criminal groups profit from sex trafficking, and force victims to engage in illicit activities including as assassins, as lookouts, and in the production, transportation, and sale of drugs. Corruption among public officials and local law enforcement, judicial, and immigration officials is a significant concern.

The US gives a Tier 2 ranking in that the Mexican government did not fully comply with the minimum standards for the illumination of human trafficking.

Brazil

CÍCERO GUEDES WAS A BRAZILIAN worker who fell victim to forced labor because of his impoverished condition. He is just one of thousands of other rural workers in Brazil enduring slavery conditions.

> "I worked hungry many times, without anything to eat. No one can work a whole day without eating a thing. My lunch was sucking on sugar cane; the suffering is marked on your face. I worked in plantations, sugar mills, factories, and the pay was next to nothing....

"I worked and worked and couldn't see any way to improve my situation. Slavery is when a person's dignity isn't respected, and when they are humiliated."[19]

Cícero is a modern-day slave.

Brazil is the largest country in South and Latin America. It is a federal presidential republic with a free market economy that in terms of Gross Domestic Product of about $2.2 billion ranks 8th in the world, slightly ahead of Italy and Russia.

Brazil imported an estimated 3.8 million slaves from Africa between the early sixteenth century and the late nineteenth century, the most of any country in the New World. That is more than nine times the number of African slaves brought to the 13 American Colonies and the United States over the same period of time.

Brazil outlawed slavery in 1888. The practice continued in remote areas into the twentieth century, but is not thought of as being widespread. However, with the expansion of ranches and farms into the Amazon in the 1960s, the demand for labor has increased, and the incidents of forced labor and slavery have increased with it.

The Walk Free Foundation's 2016 Global Slavery Index estimates that 161,100 people are victims of involuntary labor servitude in Brazil. The principal industries employing slave labor in Brazil are ranching (43 percent), deforestation (28 percent), agriculture (24 percent), logging (4 percent), and charcoal (1 percent). In 1995, Brazil's Labor Department set up the Special Mobile Inspection Group to investigate and pursue reports of forced labor and they have freed about 47,000 slave workers between 1995 and 2013. Despite these efforts, the demand for labor is increasing exponentially, and slave labor is filling the need. With 22 percent of Brazil's total population of about 208 million below the poverty line, the lure of a job is a strong magnet for poor people.

The report that interviewed Cícero above describes the flow of migrants from rural Brazil and foreign countries to urban centers in Brazil.

They came to work on the construction jobs that occurred in preparation of the World Cup in 2014 and the Olympics in 2016. The textile and garment industries in urban areas also attract prospective employees as does the sex trade. In 2013, more people were rescued from forced labor conditions in urban centers than in rural areas for the first time. According to Brazil's Ministry of Labor and Employment, 2,063 people were rescued from slave-like conditions. Of these, 1,068 had been working in urban areas. In São Paulo, the government reports that there are about 10,000 illegal sewing workshops employing some 200,000 workers, most of them immigrants.

Gil Dasio Meirelles worked in the Amazon logging trees. He worked without pay and was fed rice and beans. He was supervised by armed guards who threatened to shoot those who didn't work or tried to run away. He had been promised work and good pay, only to find himself in the middle of the 1.5 million square mile Amazon region. Many ranchers, foresters, and charcoal producers in the Amazon are out of reach of the government, and the owners impose their own laws. Meirelles devised a plan to escape.

"Three other workers helped me come up with the plan," he said. "But they got scared and backed out. They thought that if the armed guards didn't shoot us in the back, we'd be lost and starve in the jungle."

After wandering aimlessly in the jungle, Meirellas came across a road and eventually made his way to a town that had a human rights NGO. He was able to direct government forces to the work site, and the operation was closed and the landowner fined.[20]

Meirellas is a modern-day slave.

Odebrecht is a leading global construction company headquartered in Brazil. Founded in 1941, it is the largest building enterprise in Latin America, and its operations also include oil and gas, petrochemicals, weapons, and agriculture. Odebrecht has been working in Angola since

1984 and is reported to be one of the largest private employers there. In September 2015, a Brazilian court convicted the company of holding workers in conditions of slavery in an ethanol refinery construction project in Angola. The complaint accuses the company of transporting some 500 Brazilian workers to Angola for the construction of a plant that Odebrecht was building. The government alleges that the workers were deceived about the length of stay in Angola, the conditions of the work to be performed, the amount of pay to be received, and the general living conditions. If the workers complained, they were threatened with imprisonment. Their documents were confiscated and they were confined to the worksite. The complaint alleged that the Brazilian workers were treated as modern-day slaves, that they were subjected to degrading working conditions that were incompatible with human dignity, and that their freedom was curtailed.[21]

The majority of the slave workers in Brazil are debtor slaves. The workers are recruited by traffickers with the promise of good pay and lodging. They are transported to the Amazon and now to urban areas. Once at the worksite, they are told that they have incurred a debt for their travel, food, lodging, and advance, if one was offered. Their salaries often do not enable them to repay the debt and interest. The working conditions are poor. They are supervised by armed guards and threatened with violence if they do not perform the work. Their passports and documents, if they have them, are confiscated. They are locked up at night. Because they are illiterate, uneducated, impoverished, and in extremely remote areas, the possibility of escaping is nonexistent. They live in a condition of involuntary servitude, where their treatment is dehumanizing.

Brazil also has a flourishing trade in commercial sexual exploitation. According to Anti-Slavery International, approximately 70,000 Brazilian women are involved in prostitution in foreign lands. The number of prostitutes within Brazil numbers in the hundreds of thousands. The trafficking in women and children for the sex industry is controlled by organized crime and the mafias of China, Russia, Italy, Israel, and Mexico. Local officials are paid off, and the profitability of the trade invites corruption. The victims are impoverished and often from broken homes. They are promised good-paying work as nannies, domestic servants, etc., only to be sold into prostitution with a debt to be repaid for the cost incurred by the recruiter. The payment for services rendered by the prostitute go directly to the owner and are usually insufficient for repayment of the debt, especially since the debt is growing as the prostitute is charged for room and board. In other cases, women and girls are kidnapped and sold into slavery as prostitutes. Once in the foreign lands, they have no documents, cannot speak the language, and are threatened with violence or even death. They are under the total control of their masters.[22]

The US Department of State 2016 Trafficking in Persons Report ranks Brazil as a Tier 2 country. While it does not fully comply with the minimum standards for the elimination of trafficking, it is making efforts to do so. In 2012, Brazil amended its constitution to penalize those who profit from slavery through the forfeiture of their property to the federal government.

The report states that Brazil is a large source and destination country for men, women and children subjected to forced labor and sex trafficking. Child sex tourism is prevalent in resort and coastal areas in the northeast of the country. Forced labor is found on cattle ranches and in agriculture, construction, mining, logging, and charcoal production industries. Brazilian forced labor victims have been identified in other countries including Spain, Italy, and the United States.

The Walk Free Foundation's 2016 Global Slavery Index estimates the number of modern day slaves in Brazil as 161,100.

CHAPTER SEVEN

United States

THE FOLLOWING NARRATIVES, AS WELL as those in previous sections, are given to emphasize that slavery is not just an historical phenomenon or a third world issue, but a modern-day problem even within the United States.

Nicole was having a difficult time at home. Her parents were divorced, her father was absent, and she had an unsteady relationship with her mother. She was a 17-year-old high school student, and in her own words was a pretty good kid. But there was something missing in her life. So, when she met a man named Juan who gave her a lot of attention, she was charmed. She was vulnerable. It turns out the man was a pimp, and he forced her into prostitution. He used violence and beat her to prevent her from escaping. Because she didn't have any money, had no house, no car, no bank account, she was completely dependent on Juan. In her own words: "I didn't have anything. So if I left Juan, I left everything." After a severe beating, she ended up in a hospital where she met a woman who convinced her to seek help from a community service organization. Now, Nicole is free and rehabilitated, and Juan is serving a 20-year jail term.[1]

Nicole is a modern-day slave.

Ima Matul, whose story is referenced in the preface of this book, was rescued and taken to a shelter run by the Coalition to Abolish Slavery and Trafficking (CAST). The shelter provided schooling, counseling, and socialization skills. She attained a high school education, married, had three children, and now works for CAST.[2]

Ima Matul is a modern-day slave.

Holly Austin Smith was between the eighth grade and her freshman year in high school. She was experiencing the normal anxieties of a teenager and going through depression. She had met a man in a shopping mall who befriended her over a period of time. He convinced her to run away from home. Holly was 14 years old. The man turned out to be a sex trafficker, a pimp. She had little or no money, nowhere to sleep, and was very vulnerable. Within hours, she was forced into a prostitution ring in Atlantic City, New Jersey. During her time in the prostitution ring, she considered suicide. The threat or use of force kept her in the ring until she was arrested for prostitution. Initially, Holly was treated like a criminal, but eventually authorities saw her as the victim she was, and the pimp, along with two other traffickers, served a year in jail. Today, Holly is an advocate for child sex trafficking victims. She published a book in 2014 entitled *Walking Prey: How America's Youth Are Vulnerable to Sex Slavery*.[3]

Holly is a modern-day slave.

Sate Jones and Maria Jimenez were arrested near the San Francisco Airport and accused of running a sex slavery ring. They recruited young women including minors by placing ads in Bay Area newspapers promising well-paying jobs and solicited customers through an on-line website. The women were forced into a life of prostitution, threatened with violence, and deprived of food. They were given illegal drugs in order to keep awake all night to service customers. San Mateo County District Attorney Steve Wagstaffe told the *San Francisco Examiner*: "They were treated like slaves by these people."[4]

These young girls are modern-day slaves.

In May 2016 Robin Thompson was convicted of conspiring in sex trafficking of a minor. The 15-year-old girl in question was enticed from the streets of Madison, Wisconsin into a cross-country prostitution ring involving five girls. The girl was taken to Florida, Georgia, and Louisiana to provide sexual services to customers. The five girls were advertised online for sex services. They were beaten and threatened with being fed to alligators if they tried to escape. The prostitution ring was orchestrated by Robin and her husband, who is awaiting trial at the time of this writing. Robin faces up to life in prison.[5]

This teen is a modern-day slave.

In 2003, the FBI initiated Operation Cross Country as part of the Innocence Lost National Initiative, a program created to rescue child victims of sex trafficking. Through the end of 2016, the FBI has rescued approximately 6,000 sexually exploited children and obtained more than 2,500 convictions of pimps and others associated with sex trafficking, including at least 30 cases that have resulted in life sentences. Federal law enforcement officials stated that the operation is "the largest law enforcement action focused on children forced into sexual slavery." Victims reported being held against their will, beatings, assaults, and being forced into prostitution.[6]

The children forced into prostitution and rescued by Operation Cross Country are modern-day slaves.

A young woman was arrested by police in Ashland, Ohio for shoplifting a candy bar. She explained to the police that she had no money and was hungry. Upon further investigation, police learned that she was cognitively disabled and was being held against her will, made to do work for which she received no pay. When the FBI took over the investigation, they discovered that both the woman and her daughter had been enslaved for the past fourteen months by a couple, Jordie Callahan and Jessica Hunt, who lived nearby in an apartment building. The couple had enticed the mother and daughter into working for them, offering pay, lodging, and meals. Instead, they were threatened, beaten, locked in the basement or bedroom, and given only minimal food and water. They kept the daughter hostage while the mother ran chores or shopped at local stores, threatening to punish the daughter if the mother did not return or did not do the assigned work. In August 2014, Jordie Callahan was sentenced to 30 years in prison, while Jessica Hunt received a

32-year sentence on charges of labor trafficking. The woman and her daughter were freed and turned over to social services agencies.[7]

The woman and her child were modern-day slaves.

In a highly publicized case, Elizabeth Jackson was sentenced to three years in prison after pleading guilty to a single count of forced labor, and her husband pleaded guilty to harboring an alien with an expired passport. James Jackson, a former senior executive with Sony Pictures, was ordered to pay a $5,000 fine and sentenced to 200 hours of community service. The case involved a Filipino domestic servant who was brought to the United States by the couple and forced to work 16 hours a day, seven days a week. Her passport was confiscated upon arrival, and she was threatened with violence if she tried to escape. The case was tried in the US District Court in Los Angeles with the Justice Department's Civil Rights Division acting as the prosecutor. The prosecutor stated: "The Department of Justice is committed to vigorously prosecuting this type of modern-day slavery." According to the news release by the Department of Justice, its Civil Rights Division has increased by six-fold the number of human trafficking cases filed in court.[8]

Mahender Murlidhar Sabhnani and his wife, Varsha, were convicted of enslaving two Indonesian women. Mahender was from India and his wife from Indonesia, although both were naturalized United States citizens. The couple lived on Long Island, New York and ran a multi-million-dollar perfume business. They had brought two women from Indonesia to work as housekeepers five years earlier. One of the women was identified as "Samirah" in court papers. Once the women were in the United States, Mahender and Varsha confiscated their passports and threatened them with violence if they tried to escape. The women housekeepers were forced to work 18 or more hours a day and paid from $100 to $150 a month, which they never saw: the money supposedly was sent to their relatives in Indonesia. The housekeepers spoke little or no English and they were let out of the house only at night to empty the garbage. Prosecutors called it a case of modern-day slavery. These house servants were beaten, starved, and tortured. Prosecutors stated that the women were repeatedly abused, both psychologically and physically. The convicted couple were found guilty on a number of federal indictments, including forced labor, conspiracy, involuntary servitude, and harboring aliens. After the appeal process, the defendants were found guilty and Mahender was sentenced to 40 months in prison and Varsha 132 months in prison. In addition to fines, the couple had to forfeit their home to the United States.[9]

Samirah is a modern-day slave.

Nine people were indicted in Los Angeles for a sex trafficking ring that allegedly coerced young women to the United States with the promise of well-paying jobs. Once in the United States, they were forced into prostitution. The women and girls were from Guatemala, and the traffickers used witch doctors to threaten the victims with curses if they tried to escape. The victims were forced into prostitution to repay the traffickers for the cost of their transportation. The victims thus became debtor slaves. Los Angeles authorities were alerted to the ring when several of the victims escaped. Subsequently, law enforcement officials raided the targeted locations and uncovered the operation. The fifty-count indictment brought by a federal prosecutor before a grand jury alleged the ring's sex trafficking of minors; sex trafficking by force, fraud, or coercion; violating federal laws prohibiting interstate or foreign transport of minors for prostitution; importing and harboring undocumented immigrants and harboring them for prostitution; guarding women to prevent their escape; threatening their families in Guatemala; and the use of violence, force, beatings, and involuntary servitude. Robert Schoch, a special agent in charge for US Immigration and Customs Enforcement stated: "These young women were enticed into coming to this country by promises of the American Dream, only to arrive and discover that what transpired was a nightmare."[10]

In June 2002, six defendants were charged with violating the Trafficking Victims Protection Act of 2000 by trafficking forty Mexican workers to farms in New York. The defendants had lured desperate Mexican migrants from Arizona with the promise of well-paying jobs. They were transported in overcrowded vans with no seats or windows, and when they arrived at the worksite, the victims were told that they owed the defendants $1,000 for the costs incurred in their transportation. Their pay was withheld, they were supervised by armed guards, and threatened with violence. Under the Act, the penalty for conviction of forced labor carries a maximum prison term of 20 years.[11]

These workers are modern-day slaves. Many of them are also invisible slaves.

Several legal cases involving forced labor and involuntary servitude have cited violation of the Thirteenth Amendment to the United States Constitution. In 2004, in the *United States of America v. Maria Garcia*, involving slavery and involuntary servitude, the US District Court for the Western District of New York cited the Thirteenth Amendment as giving Congress the power to enact legislation to abolish slavery in the United States. The defendants had trafficked workers from Mexico and Arizona to New York as agricultural workers. The workers were not paid, told they owed the defendants money for transportation, food and lodging, threatened with violence, and held in a state of bondage.[12]

In 2001, two men in Florida were convicted of violating the Thirteenth Amendment along with other statutes and sentenced to four years in prison. They had recruited impoverished men to work on their citrus farms. Instead of paying them the promised $35–$50 a day, these two men paid only $10 a day for 12 to 14 hours of work. However, before the workers were paid, the cost of their food, lodging, and supplies was charged against their pay. As is so often true, the deductions exceeded the level of pay. If these impoverished men complained, they were threatened with violence and retribution. One of the workers did escape and informed the local police. With the help of Florida Rural Legal Services, the worker and other workers on the farm filed a lawsuit, resulting in a conviction for violating the slavery clause of the

Constitution. The perpetrators were sentenced to four years in jail.[13]

In California, Flor Molina, a former slave and human rights advocate, was instrumental in passing legislation effective January 1, 2012 that requires major manufacturers and retailers in the state to investigate and disclose what the company is doing to end human trafficking and slavery within their supply chains. The legislation is entitled California Transparency in Supply Chains Act (SB 6547). Flor testified before the state legislature about her life as a slave in the United States. She lived in Puebla, Mexico and was taking sewing lessons in the hopes of starting her own business when finishing school. Outside of school, she worked two jobs to support her three children. When she was 28 years old, her sewing teacher told her about a good-paying job in a garment factory in California. She was impoverished to the extent that, when one of her babies became ill, she did not have the money to take it to the hospital. The baby ultimately died. The job offer in the United States was very appealing, so Flor accepted the job offer and left her children with her mother. But her teacher had been approached by a trafficker. Once across the border, the trafficker took Flor's passport and clothes, placed her in a garment factory and charged her $3,000 for the "placement service." She became a debtor slave. The factory owner was an accomplice in the trafficking scheme.

Flor worked 18 hours a day sewing dresses. She had to clean the factory after the other workers left. She was fed one meal a day and slept in a storage room with another victim. She was confined to the workplace and told not to talk to the other workers. If she violated any rules or tried to escape, she was told her family back in Mexico would be punished. Flor finally convinced her employer to let her go to church. Once outside the factory, Flor contacted a legally employed legitimate co-worker, who in turn notified the FBI. The FBI directed her to CAST, where she found shelter and rehabilitation. The perpetrator was arrested and sentenced to six months' house arrest for labor abuse.

"I was enslaved for 40 days but it felt like 40 years.... I am an advocate against slavery, I am a survivor of a crime so monstrous that the only way to move forward is by fighting back. I am not the only one. There are other survivors that are fighting back with me. We are part of a group called the survivors caucus at CAST and we are working to educate people, law enforcement and communities using our stories."[14]

A brief overview of the history of slavery in the United States is crucial in placing in perspective and context the role that U.S. slavery played within global slavery.

Philip Curtin, a professor and historian on Africa and the Atlantic slave trade, published a census in 1969 that estimated that between the years 1451 and 1870 about 9.4 million African slaves entered the New World. He stated that it was unlikely that the total would fall below 7.5 million or exceed 11.3 million. Curtin estimated that about 175,000 Africans entered the Old World during this period, which includes 125,000 to the European islands off the West Coast of Africa and 50,000 to Europe. Of the total of about 9,391,000 African slaves to land in the New World over a period of about three and a half centuries, only about 4.6 percent ended up in the United States and its former colonies, according to Curtin's study.

Assuming that 10–20 percent died on the passage, the numbers shipped from Africa would fall between 8.3 to 14.8 million, according to Curtin. The number and percentage of the total is as follows:[15]

Brazil	3,647,000
Haiti	864,000
Jamaica	748,000
Cuba	702,000
Spanish South America	522,000
The Guianas	531,000
Territory of the United States	427,000

Barbados	387,000
Martinique	366,000
Leeward Islands	346,000
Guadeloupe	291,000
Mexico	200,000
Other New World	369,000

Curtin further went on in his research to summarize where the shipment of African captives ended up in the New World.

Curtin broke down the regional disembarkment of African slaves as follows:

North America	651,000	6.9%
Caribbean Islands	4,040,000	43.0%
Brazil	3,647,000	38.8%
Other South America	1,053,000	11.0%

More recent studies, including a study by the Hutchins Center for African & American Research at Harvard, estimate that 12.5 million Africans were shipped to the New World and that only 305,326 (2.4 percent) came to the United States and its former British colonies. Contrary to popular belief, The United States was a minor recipient of African slaves.[16]

While the survivor rate for the Atlantic passage is estimated at 80–90 percent, the survival rate from the capture and transport of Africans by African, Arab, and European slavers to the collection points on the African coast prior to transport to the New World was often less than 50 percent.[17]

As we have seen, the first slaves to cross the Atlantic were Arawak Native Americans Columbus brought from the New World. On his return trip from his first voyage in 1493, Columbus took seven to ten natives to the King and Queen of Spain. On his return from his second voyage in 1494, he took several hundred Arawaks back to Spain to be sold on the slave markets of the Iberian Peninsula. In the Caribbean, the Spanish enslaved local Arawak tribespeople, but they proved to be poor workers. They were also dying from disease and abuse from the Spanish. In 1501, the Spanish Crown authorized importation of African slaves who had been first "Christianized" in Spain to the New World, and in 1502, the first African slaves directly from Africa were introduced to the Spanish possessions in the Caribbean. As the indigenous American native population dwindled, the Spanish turned to Africa for the direct import of slaves to supply the labor to the New World.

The first permanent English settlement in North America dates from 1607 when the joint-stock company Virginia Company of London established the Jamestown colony with 144 men and boys. After the first year, only 38 of the original group survived. Settlers followed, and although the joint-stock company went bankrupt, the colony survived. But instead of being owned by the investors in the joint-stock company, the colony reverted to the Crown. Not finding gold, the settlers turned to growing tobacco. Tobacco is labor intensive, so more workers were required. The first workers to be brought over from Great Britain were indentured servants. At the time, many British people desired to come to the New World, either to escape religious persecution or to seek the opportunities envisioned in America. However, they did not have the funds to pay for the passage. By becoming indentured servants, they agreed to work for the employer for four to seven years and were given free ship space. The employer agreed to house and feed the employee. At the end of the work contract, the indentured servant was given freedom. To provide an incentive to the employer, the Crown deeded 50 acres of land for every indentured servant they brought over to the colony.

The first Africans to be introduced to British North America as workers arrived in 1619. In August of that year, a Dutch ship anchored at Jamestown, Virginia and sold or traded for food about 20 Africans as indentured servants. The Dutch ship had apparently raided a Spanish ship for treasure and only found the Africans. More Africans were gradually introduced to the colonies, initially as indentured servants. In 1649, a census in Virginia counted three hundred indentured servants of

African descent. Between 1619 and 1661, a gradual transformation took place whereby African indentured servant status became a condition of enslavement. Under English law, Christians were not to be enslaved and that included Christian Africans or Africans that converted to Christianity. However, that which is prohibited by law is not always followed in practice. Initially, white and black African indentured servants worked side-by-side. Once their contract was completed they were released and could and did own land. A small number of free Africans emerged. As the demand for labor outstripped the supply of white indentured servants from England, the English farmers looked to Africans from the Caribbean or Africa for workers. The indentured servant contracts of Africans were extended to the point to include life. It was not uncommon for both white and black indentured servants to run away. When caught, their length of service was increased as punishment. In one case a black African's punishment was servitude for life. Slavery was also not unknown to the colonists. It had existed for over a hundred years in the Caribbean Islands and in central and south America. Thus, gradually, a transformation occurred whereby race or skin color, instead of religion, became the deciding factor for a life of bondage.

From 1607 to the Declaration of Independence on July 4, 1776, the British North American Colonies experienced remarkable growth, and between the importation of slaves and their natural population growth, the slave population became a larger proportion of the total population. In 1671, a Virginia census found that there were about two thousand Africans and six thousand white indentured servants in a total population of forty thousand. Only a small portion of the Africans were free, thus the slave population had grown to about 5 percent of the inhabitants. By 1770, the population of the American Colonies had grown to 2.3 million, of which 462,000 were slaves—representing about 20 percent of the population.[18]

While British North America was a latecomer to the slave trade, it took advantage of it as a source of labor.

The adoption of slavery within the British colonies simply tapped into the existing slave trade network that had perfected the efficient delivery of large numbers of Africans to the Americas.[19]

From this period of increasing slave imports sprang the first protests against slavery. In 1688, Quakers in Pennsylvania protested peacefully against the practice of slavery and signed an anti-slavery petition. This "Germantown Protest" was the first formal public expression condemning slavery in the New World.[20] In 1712, the Pennsylvania assembly banned the importation of slaves, thus becoming the first of the British Colonies to prohibit the slave trade.

During the Revolutionary War, Vermont abolished slavery in 1777, Pennsylvania in 1780, and Massachusetts in 1783. By the end of the Revolutionary War in 1783, all the northern states had passed legislation to prohibit the slave trade, which meant the importation of slaves from the Caribbean or Africa. After the war, other states abolished slavery: Rhode Island and Connecticut in 1784, New York in 1785, and New Jersey in 1786.

In 1793, Eli Whitney invented the cotton gin. The cotton gin revolutionized the cotton industry as well as the plantation system and the demand for slave labor. Prior to this invention, cotton was a minor crop.

Between 1820 and 1860, the dollar value of cotton exports increased nearly nine-fold, and cotton became the dominant cash crop produced by the South. Cotton production in the South spawned a textile manufacturing industry in the North, creating a mutual dependency.

In 1808, Great Britain outlawed the transatlantic slave trade, and the United States banned the importation of slaves. These measures gave abolitionists encouragement to seek their next objective: the freeing of all slaves and the total ban on all slavers. With the slave trade banned, the primary sources of slaves were natural population growth, the illegal, clandestine importation of slaves, and domestic slave trade. Thus, while the West, led by Great Britain and several European countries, banned the slave trade and eventually slavery itself, many countries continued to practice slavery both illicitly and legally.

As the settlers moved to the West and South, in some cases taking slavery with them, the issue of where slavery would be permitted arose. In 1787, the Congress enacted the Northwest Ordinance. This ordinance banned slavery and involuntary servitude north and west of the Ohio River. It also set the conditions for statehood for the territories that comprised the Northwest Territory. In 1818, Missouri applied for statehood. Up to that point the composition of the Senate was equally balanced between free states and slave states. The Missouri Compromise of 1820 allowed Missouri to become a state with its legislature to decide whether or not to allow slavery, while Maine was to become a free state carved out of Massachusetts. The Compromise also defined where slavery would be permitted in the land acquired by the Louisiana Purchase. Land north of the 36 degrees 30 north latitude would be free while land south of the line would be open to slavery.

The Missouri Compromise of 1820 maintained a balance between free and slave states in the Senate until the end of the Mexican-American war in 1848 and the California gold rush in 1849. The Compromise of 1850 admitted California as a free state, and if and when New Mexico and Utah became states, they could choose to allow slavery or not.

The Compromise of 1850 only postponed the sectional conflicts, and the South seceded from the Union in 1861.

While slavery was banned by the Thirteenth Amendment to the Constitution in 1865, it continues into the 21st century in the United States as well as the rest of the world. The irony of this is that the United States and several Western countries that led the abolition movement, are still the subject of condemnation of having had slavery in the past by those that continue to practice it in the modern era.

CHAPTER EIGHT

Summary

T HE THIRTEENTH AMENDMENT TO THE United States Constitution was adopted in December 1865 in the latter months of the Civil War. The Amendment freed slaves in those states that were not impacted by the Emancipation Proclamation issued by Executive Order by President Abraham Lincoln on January 1, 1863. The Proclamation freed only the slaves in the ten southern states that were still in rebellion. The Amendment freed the slaves in the Border States loyal to the North and in the northern states. The Thirteenth Amendment comprises two sections and a total of two sentences.

> SECTION 1. Neither slavery nor involuntary servitude, except as a punishment for crime whereof the party shall have been duly convicted, shall exist within the United States, or any place subject to their jurisdiction.

> SECTION 2. Congress shall have power to enforce this article by appropriate legislation.

The Thirteenth Amendment does not define slavery other than by associating it with involuntary servitude. In the United States Constitution of 1788, there is no mention of slavery. To encourage the slave states to ratify the initial Constitution, reference is only made to "free people," "other persons," or "person" when referring to slaves. The South did not want the word slave or slavery mentioned in the Constitution.

After the Civil War and the Reconstruction period (1865–1877), a number of local and state regulations enabled both the state and individuals to practice continued forms of forced labor, including peonage, whereby a person is forced to work to pay off debts. Among the laws legislated by various states were the Black Codes and the Jim Crow laws. The Black Codes, a condition set by southern states for re-admittance to the Union, enabled the states to establish a separate set of laws for descendants of slaves. The Jim Crow laws imposed racial segregation at both public and private levels and "separate but equal" conditions in public schools.

Supreme Court decisions in the post-Reconstruction period largely weakened the full impact of the Thirteenth Amendment, and it was not until the mid-twentieth century that the higher court struck down the legal barriers that deprived all people of true equality. The landmark decision was the Court's ruling in *Jones v. Alfred H. Mayer Co.* in 1968. Joseph Lee Jones, an African American living in St. Louis, Missouri, sued the real estate company Alfred H. Mayer for refusing to sell a house to him because he was black. The defense claimed that Congress did not have the authority to legislate transactions between individuals. The court ruled otherwise:

> The Thirteenth Amendment ... gave Congress the power rationally to determine what are the badges and the incidents of slavery and the authority to translate that determination into effective legislation....

> ... This court recognized long ago that, whatever else they may have encompassed, the badges and incidents of slavery—its "burdens and disabilities"—included restraints upon those fundamental rights which are the essence of civil freedom, namely, the same right ... to inherit, purchase, lease, sell and convey property, as is enjoyed by white citizens.[1]

The Jones decision has allowed Congress to pass legislation that extends protection against trafficking to migrants, immigrants and all persons within the jurisdiction of the United States. The Thirteenth Amendment, in just two sentences, remains the constitutional foundation for the protection of individuals within the United States from the "badges and incidents" of involuntary servitude and trafficking and the ability of Congress to pass legislation prohibiting such action. These laws include, but are not limited to, the Mann Act of 1910 that dealt with the trafficking of women, and the Trafficking Victims Protection Act of 2000, which is comprehensive in criminalizing debtor slavery, the use of coercion, the threat of violence, and false promises or trickery which result in forced labor or involuntary servitude.

Despite the Thirteenth Amendment and the various pieces of legislation passed by Congress to enforce the Amendment as empowered by Section 2, slavery exists in the United States today as is chronicled in the opening paragraphs of this section. The prior testimonies and documentation of victims is a drop in the bucket of the extent of sex slavery, debt slavery, chattel slavery, forced labor, and involuntary servitude within the United States.

The secrecy of human trafficking makes it difficult to measure.

Percentages* of Global Forced Labor by Form

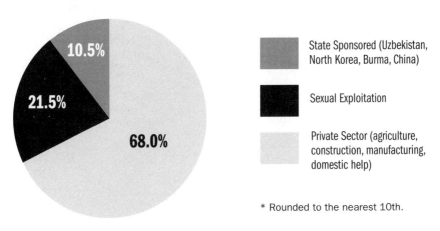

10.5% State Sponsored (Uzbekistan, North Korea, Burma, China)

21.5% Sexual Exploitation

68.0% Private Sector (agriculture, construction, manufacturing, domestic help)

* Rounded to the nearest 10th.

SOURCE: International Labor Organizationt

Annual profits of forced labor per region (US $ billion)*

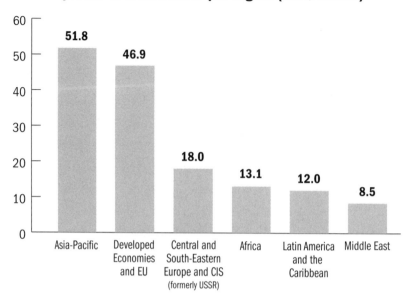

Annual profits per victim of forced labor per region (US $)*

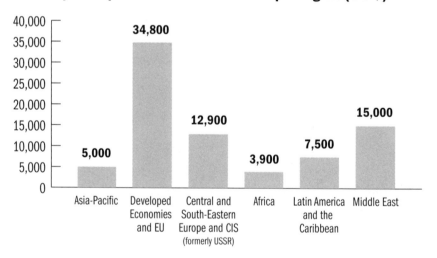

* SOURCE: International Labor Organization

Sex and forced labor trafficking is part of an underground economy, and the estimated number of victims in the United States varies widely. However, a number of experts and various governmental and non-governmental organizations have made educated estimates as to its prevalence within the United States.

In a 2000 report, the Central Intelligence Agency estimated that between 45,000 and 50,000 women and children were trafficked to the United States annually by small crime rings and loosely connected criminal networks. The victims are destined for the sex trade and forced labor. The primary source of the human cargo is Southeast Asia and Latin America, with recent trends pointing toward New Independent States and Central and Eastern Europe.[2]

A September 2004 study by Free the Slaves and the Human Rights Center at the University of California, Berkeley, entitled "Hidden Slaves: Forced Labor in the United States," states that

> Each year thousands of men, women, and children are trafficked into the United States and forced to work without pay in deplorable conditions. Hidden from view, they toil in sweatshops, brothels, farms, and private homes. To prevent them from escaping, their captors confiscate their identification documents, forbid them from leaving their workplaces or contacting their families, threaten them with arrest and deportation, and restrict their access to the surrounding community....
>
> Victims of forced labor have been tortured, raped, assaulted, and murdered. They have been held in absolute control by their captors and stripped of their dignity.[3]

Professor Oliver Kaplan, Associate Director of the Human Trafficking Center at the University of Denver, discussed human trafficking on 9 News on Denver TV:

> "There are actually very few good estimates of the total number

of people trafficked, but some estimates suggest that as many as 21 million people are in slavery, or conditions of modern-day slavery [globally]."

In his talk, he says people are trafficked into the United States for a variety of things, from forced labor, such as farm workers who work in fields, and for sex.

"Really, one of the biggest problems is that we don't have a good estimate of the prevalence of trafficking within the US."[4]

The Walk Free Foundation's 2016 Global Slavery Index estimates that there are 57,700 people enslaved within the United States, representing 0.018 percent of the population. The Walk Free Foundation estimates range between 57,000 and 63,000 people in servitude.

The State Department estimates that as many as 17,500 men, women, and children are trafficked into the United States every year. Thousands of foreigners fall victim to labor recruiters who offer the promise of well-paying jobs and amenities such as lodging and food. The recruiters pose as employment agencies and charge fees for their placement services. Instead of their dreams of glory, the victims find themselves trafficked into the sex trade or into involuntary, forced labor situations. They become debtor slaves because they cannot repay the placement fees and other costs the trafficker and employer have incurred on behalf of the victim.

According the Walk Free Foundation's 2016 Global Slavery Index, both documented and undocumented immigrants with little or no skills from Latin American and Asian countries are trafficked into the United States for use as farm hands, landscapers, janitors, cleaners, and food handlers. US children from broken homes or foster homes are vulnerable to enslavement for use as prostitutes and in forced labor situations.

Forced marriage is prevalent within the country. A US national survey in 2011 reported as many as 3,000 incidents of forced marriage within a two-year period, involving girls as young as 13. Force, fraud, or coercion was used to compel victims to marry resident foreigners or to sponsor a foreigner to enter the United States. Victims of forced marriage experience physical, psychological, and sexual abuse, obviously against their will, often associated with forced marriage.

The United States Department of State's 2016 Trafficking in Persons Report gives the country a Tier 1 ranking in that it is complying with the minimum standards for addressing the trafficking of persons and the enforcement procedures to eliminate human trafficking.

• • •

THE INTERNATIONAL LABOUR ORGANIZATION DEFINES forced labor as follows:

> Forced labour is the term used by the international community to denote situations in which persons involved—women and men, girls and boys—are made to work against their free will, coerced by their recruiter or employer, for example through violence or threats of violence, or by more subtle means such as accumulated debt, retention of identity papers or threats of denunciation to immigration authorities. Such situations can also amount to human trafficking or slavery-like practices, which are similar though not identical terms in a legal sense. International law stipulates that exacting forced labour is a crime, and should be punishable through penalties which reflect the gravity of the offence. Most countries outlaw forced labour, human trafficking and slavery-like practices in their national legislation, but successful prosecutions of offenders sadly remain few and far between.[5]

Modern-day slavery appears in four types or categories. However, the distinctions between categories are often blurred, and a slave may fall within several or all of the definitions.

Chattel slavery is perhaps the oldest form of slavery. A chattel slave is the property of the owner or master. The chattel slave is no different than an animal or other object that the master might own and can be sold, auctioned, purchased, hypothecated, or loaned. The master has total control over the slave, including the determination of life or death. Descendant-based or inherited slavery is often associated with chattel slavery. In some countries, persons who are victims of forced labor and involuntary servitude are chattel slaves. Many victims of sex slavery are chattel slaves, including harems, additional wives, and concubines. Historically, civilians and soldiers who were captives of war or insurgencies were kept or sold as slaves. That practice continues today in areas of conflict in Africa and the Middle East. Kidnapping has also been a historic source of slaves, a practice that also continues today.

Debtor slaves and victims of debt bondage and bonded labor are those that are forced into involuntary servitude because of debt burdens. The debt may have been incurred from a recruitment agency or trafficker, or from the cost of shelter and food. A person may have pledged himself or a family member as collateral for a loan. Regardless of how the loan was incurred, the work performed is insufficient to cover the interest on the loan or charges for food and shelter. The debt and pledge of work can be passed from one generation to another. The heirs become descendant-based slaves. Depending on the relationship between slave and master, the slave may also be a chattel slave. Debtor slavery or bonded labor is the most widely form of modern-day slavery.

Forced labor or involuntary servitude is another type of modern-day slavery. A person is offered a good-paying job by a trafficker or recruiter. The offer may be an advertisement in a newspaper. Upon delivery to the employer, the person finds themselves a victim of forced labor. Their documents have been confiscated and they are confined to the workplace and subject to physical abuse. They receive little or no pay. They are often in a place where they cannot speak the language. They are threatened with violence and beatings if they try to escape, as well as told that their family members back home will incur reprisals if they do not cooperate.

Victims of sex slavery, regardless of how they are sourced or recruited, end up in a situation of sexual exploitation and prostitution. As with forced labor, their documents are confiscated, they are confined to the workplace (brothel), threatened with punishment if uncooperative, and work to pay off both the debt incurred when the trafficker bought them and the increasing debt of housing, food, and interest. It is estimated that two million women and children are sold into sex slavery annually.[6]

Modern-day slavery has been labeled "the fastest-growing criminal enterprise in the world."[7] Human trafficking is the second most profitable criminal activity in the world after the illegal drug trade and ahead of the illegal firearms trade.[8] As with other criminal activities, slavery is difficult to quantify because it is part of an underground economy, takes place behind closed doors, is hidden from investigators and law enforcement and the public at large due to bribes and corrupt government officials. Also, victims are reluctant to seek help or cooperate with law enforcement due to fear of reprisals to themselves or their families. Additionally, in many societies slavery has been part of their tradition and culture for centuries, and slaveholders are unwilling to acknowledge its existence or that it is a human rights violation. Furthermore, the definitions of slavery, involuntary servitude, forced labor, and sexual exploitation are not uniformly embraced among different civilizations, societies, and cultures. Therefore, the estimates of the number of slaves vary widely among governmental surveys and human rights non-governmental organizations (NGOs).

There is no country in the world that recognizes the legal status of institutional or individual slavery today. As a legal labor system, slavery has been abolished throughout the world. However, the International Labour Organization estimates that almost 21 million people are victims of forced labor: 11.4 million women and girls and 9.5 million men and boys are victims of forced labor. Of the total people enslaved, 19 million are victims of individuals or private groups while over 2 million are victims of state or insurgency groups. Some 4.5 million people, mostly females, are subjected to forced sexual exploitation.

Forced labor in the private sector generates about $150 billion in profits to the traffickers, perpetrators, and participants. Sex trafficking is estimated to be an $8 billion international business. Some 850,000 people are trafficked across international borders annually. There are over 300,000 children who are forced into soldiering in areas of conflict around the world.[9]

Free the Slaves, an anti-slavery non-governmental organization, estimates that there are 21–30 million people in slavery around the world. They estimate that 78 percent of slave victims are in forced labor situations and 22 percent are in sex slavery.

The American Anti-Slavery Group estimates that 27 million people are currently held as chattel slaves around the world. The Walk Free Foundation estimates the number of victims of forced labor including sexual exploitation at 45.6 million. They estimate that the United States has 57,700 people in slavery. The United States Central Intelligence Agency (CIA) estimates that 14,500 to 17,000 victims of slavery are brought into the United States annually.[10]

Anti-Slavery International, the oldest human rights organization, dates back to 1839. This organization, based in London, estimates that there are over 200 million people who are victims of slavery or slavery-like conditions, although they may not qualify as pure chattel slaves. According to the United Nation's Office of the High Commission for Human Rights, one hundred million children are exploited for their labor.[11]

These estimates are more than the number of slaves in any year in the past when slavery was legally practiced.

"Trafficking" is the twenty-first century word for slave trading. It is apparently more politically correct to say "trafficking in human beings" than "slave trading." The slave trade was officially abolished by Great Britain and the United States in 1808. As with other abolished practices, the slave trade continues today (under the name of human trafficking) even though it is not legally sanctioned by any country. Trafficking is the movement of people who have been bought or sold, or the movement of people through violence, deception, or coercion from one area to another for the purpose of forced labor, slavery, or slavery-like practices. Its practice ranges from individuals acting on their own to organized crime. Traffickers use deception, trickery, coercion, violence, or the threat of violence to force people into involuntary work. Kidnapping, war, and insurgencies are also a source for trafficked peoples. The victim, or person trafficked, ends up owing the trafficker for the cost of the transportation, food, clothing, shelter, and other items. The person is sold to a buyer who then creates a debt that the person has to pay back. Often, the debt grows as the creditor charges for food, shelter, and other items plus interest. The debtor becomes the slave of the owner. If the trafficked person has legal papers, they are confiscated by the employer. The slave has been purchased, the slave is working against his or her will, the threat or actual use of violence breaks the will of the slave and assures compliance and the slave's movements are controlled. The slave's wages, if any, are controlled by the master. Most of contemporary slavery is debtor or bonded slavery. Most of the victims are women and children.

There are documented reports of slavery taking place on all six continents. Bonded slavery is prevalent in the cocoa farms of West Africa, the carpet-making factories in India, Pakistan, Nepal, and Bangladesh and the ranching, agriculture, logging, and charcoal industries of Brazil. Forced labor camps are prevalent in China and North Korea. Women, men, and children are rescued every year in the United States from forced labor and sex slavery situations in brothels, domestic work, construction, food service, as well as the farming and garment industries. Virtually every country in the world has bonded domestic servants. Many girls and women in all countries are forced into prostitution to repay debts incurred in fleeing their impoverished countries. Women and girls captured in armed conflicts in Nigeria, Syria, Iraq, and several central

African nations are held as slaves or sold into slavery.

Slavery by Europeans in the New World that emanates from the first voyage of Columbus to the Atlantic slave trade and was part of every geographic sector of the Western Hemisphere was not a creation of the "West." It was a practice that originated with the advent of agriculture and animal husbandry beginning with the end of the last ice age, about twelve thousand years ago. However, the West and particularly the United States are condemned for embracing the institution, even though slavery had a long history in the Old World going back to the earliest of times. While the practice of slavery should not in any way be excused, it was legally and morally accepted by virtually all societies, cultures and civilizations prior to the settlement of the New World by Europeans; indeed, it was practiced in the Americas before European immigration by indigenous Native American tribes. But it was the Western abolitionist movement that began to free the slaves, not only in the Americas but also throughout the rest of the world. Slavery was an evil, and still is, and the laws and regulations to end it were initiated by the British and other European powers and the United States. Although it is still practiced in almost every country, these Western countries led the way for ending slavery as a legal practice.

England engendered the abolition cause in the late eighteenth century with Lord Mansfield's ruling in 1772 that slaves were free when they entered Britain. A concurrent movement was underway in the United States. Denmark outlawed the slave trade in 1803 and both the British and the United States outlawed the slave trade beginning in 1808. Great Britain outlawed slavery in all its colonies in the West Indies, South Africa and Mauritius in 1834, to be finalized in 1838 through a system of apprenticeship, and the United States abolished slavery in 1865. In the New World, the freeing of slaves rolled through the various countries, with Brazil in 1888 being the last country to free its slaves.

Prodded by the Europeans, the abolition movement spread through Asia, Africa, and the Middle East. The last countries to abolish slavery were Saudi Arabia and Yemen in 1962 and Niger in Africa in 2004. However, as we have seen, the illegal slave trade continues in every country into the twenty-first century.

Western Civilization and the United States did not invent slavery, but they did lead the way to end it as a legal institution. Nevertheless, as discussed in this book, slavery exists throughout the world today, even though it is outlawed in virtually every country. Because it is profitable for the perpetrators, slavery draws organized crime gangs, and targets through deception, coercion, force and subjection susceptible and vulnerable victims who are in need of work and looking for a well-paying job.

Throughout this book the victims of slavery have told their stories. We have been privy to many of the victims' stories as well as the stories of the perpetrators. We have seen how the traffickers work, how the accomplices in local, county, state, and federal governments accept bribes to look the other way.

What Can You Do?

MOST MODERN-DAY SLAVES, PARTICULARLY in the household help and sex trafficking industries, are invisible slaves. Many other slaves are in remote areas, not visible to the average person and, therefore, the average person is not aware that slavery exists to the extent that it does.

What are the remedies to combating modern-day slavery? The first is awareness. It is the purpose of this book to bring awareness to how wide-spread human trafficking is currently. So awareness means:

BE AWARE OF what goes on in your neighborhood and report to local law enforcement agencies any suspicious activity.

HOLD YOUR LOCAL, state, and federal officials accountable for enforcing the laws against human trafficking.

TELL YOUR ELECTED representatives to enforce sanctions against foreign countries that receive a poor review from the Department of

State's annual Trafficking Victims Protection Act.

WRITE TO THEM to let them know that you are concerned about human trafficking and what are they doing about it.

ENCOURAGE YOUR LOCAL schools to introduce knowledge of human trafficking into the curriculum so that students may learn how vulnerable young children are to traffickers.

ENCOURAGE YOUR FRIENDS and associates to become involved in spreading the word about modern-day human trafficking.

DONATE TIME AS a volunteer or money to local, county, state, federal, and international non-governmental organizations that are fighting slavery and supporting victims.

BE AWARE OF what you buy and boycott goods or services that come from countries tainted with products that are produced from slave or child labor.

WRITE TO COMPANIES that may have supply chains that are vulnerable to human trafficking. The Department of Labor publishes a List of Goods Produced by Child Labor or Forced Labor that can be helpful in promoting people to become conscientious consumers.

Awareness is essential to helping to mitigate modern-day slavery. Create an atmosphere that exposes the invisible slave to a visible slave. Then report to your local, county, state, or federal authority any and all suspicious activity.

Acknowledgments

MANY PEOPLE CAME TOGETHER TO make this work possible. Their encouragement as to the importance of the subject—modern-day slavery—prodded me to keep going during the times I felt challenged. They kept me focused on the goal of the project: to bring awareness to the scope of twenty-first-century slavery.

This book would not exist if not for my wife, Julie. I had been working on a larger subject, the history of slavery, when she directed my attention to the issue of modern-day slavery and urged me to address that problem. She labored through numerous rounds of reading and editing; her devotion to the book was unending. Thank you, Julie.

Various people read drafts and offered helpful comments and feedback. Jack Mosbacker was invaluable in the early stages of writing, both to organizing the material and its presentation. Jacqueline Gilman, the book designer, was the quarterback of the team that brought the completed manuscript to the publisher. This group worked in unison and harmony to integrate edits, endnotes, bibliography, images, corrections, and comments. The group included, in addition to Jacqueline, editors Jim Baldwin and Maura Harris. Jerome Handler of the Virginia Foundation of the Humanities was helpful in providing me access to its library and archival collection of slavery images, as was Lisa Kristine and her fine work as a modern-day abolitionist and her collection of images. A number of people outside the production team agreed to read and offer comments on the book including Ken and Rebecca Jowitt, Tom Henriksen, Theresa Duran, and Ayaan Hirsi Ali.

Chris Dauer introduced me to the Hoover Press, which brought the end product to the public. Its level of professionalism is unmatched. The Hoover Press is headed by Barbara Arellano; her team that produced the book includes Marshall Blanchard, Scott Harrison, Laura Somers, and Jennifer Navarrette. Thank you for making all this possible.

All the research on the book originated with the author; despite my best efforts to vet and confirm the sources of references, any and all errors reside with me.

W. Kurt Hauser

Appendix I

The following is a list of Non-Governmental Organizations that combat slavery.

100x Development Foundation
7020 Fain Park Drive, Suite 6
Montgomery, AL 36117
100xdevelopement.com
334-387-1178

Anti-Slavery International
Thomas Clarkson House
The Stableyard, Broomgrove Road
London, SW9 9TL, UK
info@antislavery.org
44-20-7501-8920

10ThousandWindows
348 North Canyons
Livermore, CA 94551
10thousandwindows.org
925-579-5426

Abolish Child Trafficking (ACT) Covenant House
461 8th Avenue
New York, NY 10001
abolishchildtrafficking.org
800-388-3888

Breaking Free
PO Box 4366
Saint Paul, MN 55104
breakingfree.net
651-645-6557

Child Labor Coalition
1320 19th Street NW, Ste. 600
Washington, DC 20036
stopchildlabor.org
reidm@nclnet.org
202-775-7408

CNN Freedom Project
Atlanta, GA 30303
cnn.com/specials/world/freedom-project
404-827-1500

Coalition to Abolish Slavery and Trafficking (CAST)
5042 Wilshire Blvd., Ste. 586
Los Angeles, CA 90036
info@castla.org
213-365-1906

Free the Slaves
1320 19th Street NW
Washington, DC 20036
info@freetheslaves.net
202-775-7480

Human Rights Watch
350 5th Avenue, 34 floor
New York, NY 10118
hrwpress@hrw.org
212-290-4700

iAbolish, American Anti-Slavery Group
198 Tremont Street, #421
Boston, MA 02116
iabolish.org
888-373-7888

International Justice Mission
PO Box 58147
Washington, DC 20037
ijm.org
703-465-5495

International Rescue Committee
122 East 42nd Street
New York, NY 10168
rescue.org
316-351-5495

National Immigrant Justice Center
208 LaSalle Street, Ste. 1300
Chicago, IL 60604
immigrantjustice.org
888-373-7888

Polaris Project
PO Box 65323
Washington, DC 20035
polarisproject.org
info@polarisproject.org
202-745-1001

Project Rescue
PO Box 922
Springfield, MS 65801
projectrescue.com
417-833-5564

Restavek Freedom
11160 Kenwood Road, Ste. 200
Cincinnati, OH 45242
restavekfreedom.org
513-475-3710

Stop the Traffik
Second Floor, Oasis Hub
1A Kennington Road
London, SE1 7QP, UK
stopthetraffik.org/uk
44 (0) 207-921-4258

The Walk Free Foundation
PO Box 3155
Broadway Nedlands, W. Australia 6009
info@walkfreefoundation.org
618 6460 4949

Wilberforce Institute for the Study of Slavery and Emancipation
University of Hull
Oriel Chambers
27 High Street
Hull, England, HU1 1NE, UK
www2.hull.ac.uk
44-0-1482-305176

Appendix II

Law enforcement agencies in the United States that are involved in efforts to combat human trafficking:

The Civil Rights Division's Human Trafficking Prosecution Unit, the Executive Office for US Attorneys, and several US Attorney Offices (USAO) lead Anti-Trafficking Coordination Teams (ACTeams) in collaboration with the Federal Bureau of Investigation (FBI), The Department of Homeland Security (DHS), Immigration and Customs Enforcement (ICE), and the Department of Labor (DOL). The FBI recognizes the most effective way to investigate human trafficking is in a collaborative, multi-agency environment. To foster such an approach, the FBI leads or participates in over 100 human trafficking task forces and working groups.

The Federal Bureau of Investigation's (FBI's) Innocence Lost National Initiative addresses the growing problem of children recruited into prostitution. This initiative is in partnership with Department of Justice (DOJ) Child Exploitation and Obscenity Section (CEOS), and the National Center for Missing and Exploited Children (NCMEC).

Office of Juvenile Justice and Delinquency Prevention (OJJDP) and its grantee, **Girls Educational Mentoring Services (GEMS),** provides training to OJJDP-funded Internet Crimes Against Children (ICAC) Task Forces in an effort to build capacity of ICAC Task Forces to respond to domestic minor sex trafficking.

The Bureau of Justice Assistance (BJA) and **Office for Victims of Crime (OVC)** jointly award funding to support Enhanced Collaborative Model Task Force sites through the Enhanced Collaborative Model to Combat Human Trafficking.

Bureau of Indian Affairs (BIA)—Division of Drug Enforcement (DDE) works in collaboration with other federal, state, tribal, and local entities on human trafficking investigations. BIA is working with other partners to multiply forces to combat the growing human trafficking problem in and around Indian Country.

DOL's Wage and Hour Division (WHD) and Office of Inspector General (OIG) have continued to participate in the Federal Enforcement Working Group, and are actively working alongside law enforcement partners in pilot ACTeams. WHD plays a key role in these interagency efforts by assisting the law enforcement agencies that are developing and prosecuting human trafficking cases. For example, WHD computes back wages and liquidated damages for the victims, reviews employer records, and provides translation services where necessary, as well as helping to identify potential trafficking cases in the course of regular WHD investigations. The OIG investigates fraud and abuse related to DOL's Foreign Labor Certification (FLC) Programs (PERM, H-2A, H-1B, H-2B, etc.), as well as non-traditional organized crime threats that may jeopardize the integrity of these FLC programs.

WHD is also participating in DOJ-funded task forces that are operating in a number of states. These task forces, composed of both federal law enforcement agencies and NGOs, are working to strengthen domestic trafficking investigations and prosecutions.

ICE has designated a number of specially trained human trafficking subject matter experts—at least one in every ICE HSI Special Agent in Charge (SAC) field office. These individuals are trained to handle human trafficking leads, address urgent victim needs appropriately, and serve as designated points of contact for local officers and leads.

Each **USAO** across the country is leading or participating in an anti-human trafficking task force. The USAO task forces include those that are operational and focus on criminal investigation and prosecution and those that address related issues, such as regional coordination and information-sharing and trafficking victims' unique needs. Task forces also engage in training public awareness activities, as well. Task force membership generally includes federal law enforcement partners, state and local law enforcement, and various NGOs, including those providing victim services. In addition, some task forces also include tribal law enforcement, community and faith-based organizations, legal aid, and child and family service organizations. Further, most of the USAOs employ a comprehensive spectrum approach in their task force participation; in addition to the US Attorney, participants from the USAOs may include prosecutors, law enforcement coordinators, and victim assistance personnel.

The Executive Office for U.S. Attorneys' National Advocacy Center, with the assistance of the CEOS Section, periodically holds the Project Safe Childhood Advanced Online Child Exploitation Seminar. Significant focus is placed on the investigation and prosecution of child exploitation offenses that were, as of that time, recently incorporated into the Project Safe Childhood initiative, including domestic prostitution of minors and sexual exploitation of children who were outside the United States.

The Executive Office for U.S. Attorneys holds a Working with Victims of Violent Crimes and Civil Rights Crime Seminar for USAO Victim-Witness personnel. Included on the agenda are sessions about resources for human trafficking victims and strategies for human trafficking case management, including partnering with NGOs.

Since 2003, the FBI has partnered with **National Centre for Missing and Exploited Children (NCMEC)** to host the Protecting Victims of Child Prostitution training course. Over 1,350 law enforcement officers and prosecutors have received this training on the comprehensive identification, intervention, and investigation of the commercial sexual exploitation of children.

ODDJP funds seminars involving the National Center for Juvenile and Family Court Judges focusing on the role of courts in addressing the needs of victims of domestic child sex trafficking. This roundtable informs the development of a judicial curriculum and tools to better identify victims of domestic child sex trafficking already involved with the juvenile and family court systems.

Notes

Preface

1. Steve Hargreaves, "I Was a Modern-Day Slave in America," *CNN Money*, November 25, 2013, http://money.cnn.com/2013/11/21/news/economy/human-trafficking-slave/.
2. Walk Free Foundation, *The Global Slavery Index 2016* (Perth, Australia: Minderoo Foundation, 2016), http://assets.globalslaveryindex.org/downloads/Global+Slavery+Index+2016.pdf.
3. International Labor Organization; freetheslaves.net facts and figures.
4. International Labor Organization; freetheslaves.net facts and figures.

Chapter One: An Ancient Institution

1. This subject is addressed in Patrick Manning, *Slavery and African Life: Occidental, Oriental, and African Slave Trades* (Cambridge: Cambridge University Press, 1990).
2. James F. Nihan, *World Slavery: A Documented History* (Laguna Hills, CA: Aegean Park Press, 1999); Junius P. Rodriguez, *The Historical Encyclopedia of World Slavery* (Santa Barbara, CA: ABC-CLIO, 1997); Seymour Drescher and Stanley L. Engerman, eds., *A Historical Guide to World Slavery* (New York: Oxford University Press, 1998).
3. Deut. 5:15.
4. Aristotle, *Politics*, Book 3, trans. Benjamin Jowett (n.p.: Classics-Unbound, 2008).
5. Ibid., Book 3.
6. Ibid., Book 5.
7. David Livingstone, *The Last Journals of David Livingstone, in Central Africa, from 1865 to His Death*, vol. 2, *1869–1873*, ed. Horace Waller (London: John Murray, 1874), pp. 76–77.
8. *Dred Scott v. John F. A. Sandford*, 60 US (19 How.) 393 (1857), https://supreme.justia.com/cases/federal/us/60/393/case.html.
9. Manning, *Slavery and African Life*, pp. 102–107.
10. Noah Webster and Jean L. McKechnie, *Webster's New Universal Unabridged Dictionary*, 2nd ed. (n.p.: Dorset & Baber, 1979).
11. 1 Cor. 12:13.
12. *Webster's New Universal Unabridged Dictionary*.
13. Aristotle, *Politics*, Books 1 and 2.

14. Thomas Wiedemann, *Greek and Roman Slavery* (London: Routledge, 1994), p. 15.

15. As an interesting aside, this reference in the Thirteenth Amendment is the only use of the word "slave" or "slavery" in the US Constitution.

16. Office of the United Nations High Commissioner for Human Rights (OHCHR), Slavery Convention, 25 September 1926, Article 1 (1), http://www.ohchr.org/EN/ProfessionalInterest/Pages/Slavery Convention.aspx.

17. Ibid., Article 1 (2).

18. Office of the United Nations High Commissioner for Human Rights (OHCHR), Supplementary Convention on the Abolition of Slavery, the Slave Trade, and Institutions and Practices Similar to Slavery, 30 April 1956, Article 1 (a)–(d), http://www.ohchr.org/EN/Profession-alInterest/Pages/SupplementaryConventionAbolitionOfSlavery.aspx.

19. Swathi Mehta, "A Report on Debt Bondage, Carpet-Making, and Child Slavery," iAbolish.org, 2010, http://www.iabolish.org/index.php?option=com_content&id=184:a-report-on-debt-bondage-carpet-making-and-child-slavery-&Itemid=8.

20. International Labour Organization, "ILO 2012 Global Estimate of Forced Labour Executive Summary" (Geneva: International Labour Organization, ILO Special Action Programme to Combat Forced Labour [SAP-FL], Programme for the Promotion of the Declaration of Fundamental Principles and Rights at Work, 2012), http://www.ilo.org/wcmsp5/groups/public/---ed_norm/---declaration/documents/publication/wcms_181953.pdf.

21. US Department of State, Office of the Under Secretary for Democracy and Global Affairs and Bureau of Public Affairs, "The 2009 Trafficking in Persons (TIP) Report," US Department of State Publication 11407, revised June 2009, https://www.state.gov/documents/organization/123357.pdf.

22. James W. C. Pennington, *The Fugitive Blacksmith* (London: Charles Gilpin, 1849), pp. 10, 14, quoted in Walter Johnson, *Soul by Soul: Life Inside the Antebellum Slave Market* (Cambridge, MA: Harvard University Press, 1999), p. 218.

23. Orlando Patterson, *Slavery and Social Death: A Comparative Study* (Cambridge, MA: Harvard University Press, 1982), p. 7.

24. There are very few surviving written documents by slaves describing their experiences. Douglass, in addition to other writings, authored an autobiography. See Frederick Douglass, *Narrative of the Life of Frederick Douglass, an American Slave, Written by Himself*, ed. Benjamin Quarles (Cambridge, MA: Harvard University Press, 1960).

25. Frederick Douglass, *My Bondage and My Freedom*, ed. John David Smith (New York: Penguin Books, 2003), pp. 30, 32, 41.

26. Harriet A. Jacobs, *Incidents in the Life of a Slave Girl, Written by Herself* (Cambridge, MA: Harvard University Press, 1987), pp. 135, 106.

27. Mende Nazer and Damien Lewis, *Slave: My True Story* (New York: Public Affairs, 2003), p. 140.

28. Shyima Hall and Lisa Wysocky, *Hidden Girl: The True Story of a Modern-Day Child Slave* (New York: Simon & Schuster BFYR, 2014), pp. 39–40.

29. Pierre Dan, *Histoire de Barbarie et de ses Corsaires* (Paris, 1637), p. 277, as quoted in Bernard Lewis, *The Middle East: A Brief History of the Last 2,000 Years* (New York: Touchstone, 1995), p. 175.

30. Plato, *Laws* 776c–d.

31. Homer, *The Odyssey* 17:322.

32. Jacobs, *Incidents in the Life of a Slave Girl*, p. 28.

33. Douglass, *My Bondage and My Freedom*, p. 191.

34. Hall and Wysocky, *Hidden Girl*, p. 47.

35. Jan R. Carew, quoted in Richard Brent Turner, *Islam in the African-American Experience*, 2nd ed. (Bloomington: Indiana University Press, 2003), p. 11.

36. Jonathan Curiel, "The Life of Omar ibn Said," *Aramco World* 61, no. 2 (March/April 2010): 36.

37. Turner, *Islam in the African-American Experience*, p. xvii.

38. Paul E. Lovejoy, *Transformations in Slavery: A History of Slavery in Africa*, 3rd ed. (New York: Cambridge University Press, 2012), p. 270.

39. Michael Specter, "Contraband Women—A Special Report: Traffickers' New Cargo: Naive Slavic Women," *New York Times*, January 11, 1998, http://www.nytimes.com/1998/01/11/world/contraband-women-a-special-report-traffickers-new-cargo-naive-slavic-women.html.

Chapter Two: Modern-Day Slavery

1. International Labour Organization, "Forced Labour, Modern Slavery, and Human Trafficking," http://www.ilo.org/global/topics/forced-labour/lang--en/index.htm, accessed October 7, 2014.

2. Walk Free Foundation, *The Global Slavery Index 2016* (Perth, Australia: Minderoo Foundation, 2016), http://assets.globalslaveryindex.org/downloads/Global+Slavery+Index+2016.pdf.

3. Free the Slaves, "About Slavery: Slavery Today," http://www.freetheslaves.net/about-slavery/slavery-today/.

Chapter Three: Middle East

1. Robert Fulford, "Slavery's Modern Face in the Middle East," *National Post* (Ontario), August 16, 2014, http://news.nationalpost.com/full-comment/robert-fulford-slaverys-modern-face-in-the-middle-east.

2. Walk Free Foundation, *The Global Slavery Index 2016* (Perth, Australia: Minderoo Foundation, 2016), http://assets.globalslaveryindex.org/downloads/Global+Slavery+Index+2016.pdf.

3. Ibid.

4. Shyima Hall and Lisa Wysocky, *Hidden Girl: The True Story of a Modern-Day Child Slave* (New York: Simon & Schuster BFYR, 2014), p. 1.

5. Ibid., p. 20.

6. Seth J. Frantzman, "Sisi, Crack Down on Mass Murder, Torture in Sinai!," *The Jerusalem Post*, June 22, 2014, http://www.jpost.com/Opinion/Columnists/Sisi-crack-down-on-mass-murder-torture-in-Sinai-360204.

7. Ibid.

8. Will Durant, *The Story of Civilization*, vol. 2, *The Life of Greece* (New York: Simon and Schuster, 1966), p. 596. See also Gustave Glotz, *Ancient Greece at Work: An Economic History from the Homeric Period to the Roman Conquest*, trans. M. R. Dobie (New York: Routledge, 1926), p. 356; W. W. Tarn, *Hellenistic Civilisation* (London: E. Arnold & Company, 1927), p. 204.

9. Yvon Garlan, *Slavery in Ancient Greece*, trans. Janet Lloyd (New York: Cornell University Press, 1988), p. 145; Diodorus Siculus, *Library of History, Volume II, Books 2.35–4.58*, trans.

C. H. Oldfather, Loeb Classical Library 303 (Cambridge, MA: Harvard University Press, 1935), Book 3, chapters 12–14, pp. 6–7, https://www.loebclassics.com/view/LCL303/1935/volume.xml.

10. US Department of State, Office of the Under Secretary for Civilian Security, Democracy, and Human Rights, "The 2016 Trafficking in Persons (TIP) Report," June 2016, https://www.state.gov/documents/organization/258876.pdf.

11. Ibid.

12. Amnesty International, "'My Sleep Is My Break': Exploitation of Migrant Domestic Workers in Qatar," http://www.amnestyusa.org/pdfs/mde220042014en.pdf, pp. 5–6.

13. Ibid., pp. 47–49.

14. US Central Intelligence Agency, "Middle East: Qatar," in *The World Factbook*, https://www.cia.gov/library/publications/the-world-factbook/geos/qa.html.

15. US Department of Energy, Energy Information Administration (EIA), "Total Petroleum and Other Liquids Production—2015," http://www.eia.gov/countries/cab.cfm?fips=qa.

16. Al-Alam News Network, "Int'l Delegation Decries Qatar Modern Slavery," December 2, 2013, http://en.alalam.ir/news/1540550.

17. Ibid.

18. *Annual Report of the National Human Rights Committee on the Situation of Human Rights in the State of Qatar (2011)*, http://www.nhrc-qa.org/wpcontent/uploads/2014/01/NHRC-Annual-Report-A-2011.pdf, p. 50.

19. Walk Free Foundation, *Global Slavery Index 2016*.

20. Daniel Greenfield, "Saudi Offers 'Castrated African Slave' for Sale on Facebook," *FrontPage Magazine*, November 30, 2012, http://www.frontpagemag.com/2012/dgreenfield/saudi-offers-castrated-african-slave-for-sale-on-facebook/.

21. Ruth Sherlock, "Saudi Prince Who Killed Manservant 'to Be Allowed Home,'" *The Telegraph*, November 13, 2012, http://www.telegraph.co.uk/news/uknews/crime/9674420/Saudi-prince-who-killed-manservant-to-be-allowed-home.html.

22. Human Rights Watch, "World Report 2012: Saudi Arabia; Events of 2011," http://www.hrw.org/world-report-2012/world-report-2012-saudi-arabia.

23. Samuel Oakford, "As the Saudis Covered Up Abuses in Yemen, America Stood By," *Politico Magazine*, July 30, 2016, http://www.politico.com/magazine/story/2016/07/saudi-arabia-yemen-russia-syria-foreign-policy-united-nations-blackmail-214124.

24. Anti-Slavery International, "Trafficking in Women: Forced Labour and Domestic Work in the Context of the Middle East and Gulf Region," Working Paper, 2006, http://www.antislavery.org/includes/documents/cm_docs/2009/t/traffic_women_forced_labour_domestic_2006.pdf.

25. Jennifer Daddario, "Human Trafficking 'World-Wide Epidemic,'" *Cleveland Jewish News*, April 26, 2007, http://www.cleveland-jewishnews.com/archives/human-trafficking-world-wide-epidemic/article_f46d00bc-72e7-543d-a457-e9f5403ab1aa.html.

26. Halil Inalcik, "Servile Labor in the Ottoman Empire," in *The Mutual Effects of the Islamic and Judeo-Christian Worlds*, ed. A. Ascher, T. Halasi-Kun, and B. K. Kiraly (New York: Brooklyn College Press, 1979), pp. 25–43.

27. Bernard Lewis, *Race and Slavery in the Middle East: An Historical Enquiry* (New York: Oxford University Press, 1992), p. 72.

28. Ronald Segal, *Islam's Black Slaves: The Other Black Diaspora* (New York: Farrar, Straus and Giroux, 2001), p. 149.

29. Uzay Bulut, "ISIS Selling Yazidi Women and Children in Turkey," Gatestone Institute, December 20, 2015, https://www.gatestoneinstitute.org/7078/turkey-isis-slaves.

30. "Rights Violations, Terror Ops Threaten Turkey's Democratic Institutions: PACE," *Hürriyet Daily News*, June 23, 2016, http://www.hurriyetdailynews.com/rights-violations-terror-ops-threaten-turkeys-democratic-institutions-pace.aspx-?pageID=238&nID=100835&NewsCatID=339.

31. European Stability Initiative (ESI), "The Great Debate: Germany, Turkey, and the Turks; Part I: Intellectuals," October 2010, http://www.esiweb.org/pdf/The%20Great%20Debate%20-%20Germany,%20Turkey%20and%20the%20Turks%20-%20Part%201%20-%20Intellectuals%20-%20October%202010.pdf, p. 6.

32. US Central Intelligence Agency, "Middle East: United Arab Emirates, in *The World Factbook*, https://www.cia.gov/library/publications/the-world-factbook/geos/ae.html.

33. Walk Free Foundation, *Global Slavery Index 2016*.

34. Ibid.

35. US Department of State, Office of the Under Secretary for Democracy and Global Affairs and Bureau of Public Affairs, "The 2009 Trafficking in Persons (TIP) Report," US Department of State Publication 11407, revised June 2009, https://www.state.gov/documents/organization/123357.pdf.

Chapter Four: Africa

1. Anti-Slavery International, "Trafficking of Children in West Africa—Focus on Mali and Côte d'Ivoire," June 2001, http://web.archive.org/web/20010501040155/http://www.anti-slavery.org/archive/other/trafficking-children-wafrica.htm.

2. As quoted in Junius P. Rodriquez, *The Historical Encyclopedia of World Slavery*, vol. 1 (Oxford: ABC-CLIO, 1997), p. 305.

3. Mende Nazer and Damien Lewis, *Slave: My True Story* (New York: Public Affairs, 2003), p. 140.

4. Ibid., p. 154.

5. It was published in 2003; see note 3.

6. Jesse Sage and Liora Kasten, eds., *Enslaved: True Stories of Modern Day Slavery* (New York: Palgrave Macmillan, 2006), p. 45.

7. Ibid., p. 51.

8. Jonathan Gelbart, "Genocide in the First Person: An Interview with Simon Deng," *Stanford Review Online Edition* 40, No. 4 (February 24, 2008), http://www.stanfordreview.org/old_archives/Archive/Volume_XL/Issue_4/Features/features1.shtml.

9. *Wall Street Journal*, August 19, 2016, p. A12.

10. Walk Free Foundation, *The Global Slavery Index 2016* (Perth, Australia: Minderoo Foundation, 2016), http://assets.globalslavery-index.org/downloads/Global+Slavery+Index+2016.pdf.

11. Walk Free Foundation, *The Global Slavery Index 2014* (Claremont: Hope for Children Organization Australia, 2014), http://assets.globalslaveryindex.org/content/uploads/2016/08/30110259/2014-Global-Slavery-Index.pdf.

12. US Department of State, Office of the Under Secretary for Civilian Security, Democracy, and Human Rights, "The 2016 Trafficking in Persons (TIP) Report," June 2016, https://www.state.gov/documents/organization/258876.pdf.

13. Nazer and Lewis, *Slave*, p. 187.

14. Ibid., p. 200.

15. Annie Kelly, "Sexual Slavery Rife in Democratic Republic of the Congo, Says MSF," *The Guardian*, July 23, 2014, https://www.theguardian.com/global-development/2014/jul/23/sexual-slavery-democratic-republic-congo-msf.

16. Free the Slaves, "Congo's Mining Slaves: Enslavement at South Kivu Mining Sites," Investigative Report, June 2013, https://www.freetheslaves.net/wp-content/uploads/2015/03/Congos-Mining-Slaves-web-130622.pdf.

17. US Department of State, "2016 Trafficking in Persons (TIP) Report."

18. Michael Finkel, "Is Youssouf Malé a Slave?," *New York Times Magazine*, November 18, 2001, http://www.nytimes.com/2001/11/18/magazine/is-youssouf-male-a-slave.html.

19. US Central Intelligence Agency, "Africa: Cote D'Ivoire," in *The World Factbook*, https://www.cia.gov/library/publications/the-world-factbook/geos/iv.html; Food Empowerment Project, "Child Labor and Slavery in the Chocolate Industry," http://www.foodispower.org/slavery-chocolate/.

20. US Central Intelligence Agency, "Africa: Cote D'Ivoire."

21. US Department of State, "2016 Trafficking in Persons (TIP) Report."

22. David McKenzie and Brent Swails, "Child Slavery and Chocolate: All Too Easy to Find," The CNN Freedom Project (blog), January 19, 2012, http://thecnnfreedomproject.blogs.cnn.com/2012/01/19/child-slavery-and-chocolate-all-too-easy-to-find/.

23. US Department of State, "2016 Trafficking in Persons (TIP) Report."

24. Sage and Kasten, *Enslaved*, pp. 177–203.

25. John D. Sutter, "Slavery's Last Stronghold," March 16, 2012, http://www.cnn.com/interactive/2012/03/world/mauritania.slaverys.last.stronghold/index.html.

26. Ibid.

27. U.S Department of State, Bureau of Democracy, Human Rights, and Labor, "Country Reports on Human Rights Practices for 2013: Mauritania," http://www.state.gov/j/drl/rls/hrrpt/humanrightsreport/index.htm?year=2013&dlid=220136.

28. US Department of State, Office of the Under Secretary for Civilian Security, Democracy, and Human Rights, "The 2014 Trafficking

in Persons (TIP) Report: Mauritania," June 2014, https://www.state.gov/j/tip/rls/tiprpt/countries/2014/226775.htm.

29. US Central Intelligence Agency, "Africa: Niger," in *The World Factbook*, https://www.cia.gov/library/publications/ the-world-factbook/geos/ng.html.

30. Ibn Battuta, *Travels in Asia and Africa 1325–1354*, trans. and ed. H. A. R. Gibb (London: Broadway House, 1929), pp. 113–115.

31. Walk Free Foundation, *Global Slavery Index 2016*.

32. Galy Kadir Abdelkader and Moussa Zangaou, "Wahaya: Domestic and Sexual Slavery in Niger," published by Anti-Slavery International and Timidria, 2012, http://www.antislavery.org/includes/ documents/cm_docs/2012/w/wahaya_report_eng.pdf.

33. US Department of State, "2016 Trafficking in Persons (TIP) Report."

34. US Department of State, Office of the Under Secretary for Civilian Security, Democracy, and Human Rights, "The 2014 Trafficking in Persons (TIP) Report: Niger," June 2014, http://www.state.gov/j/tip/rls/tiprpt/countries/2014/226789.htm.

35. X. S., "Slavery in Niger: A First Conviction," *Economist*, June 2, 2014, http://www.economist.com/blogs/baobab/2014/06/slavery-niger?zid=304&ah=e5690753dc78ce91909083042ad12e30.

36. US Central Intelligence Agency, "Africa: Nigeria," in *The World Factbook*, https://www.cia.gov/library/publications/resources/ the-world-factbook/geos/ni.html.

37. Walk Free Foundation, *Global Slavery Index 2016*.

38. US Department of State, "2016 Trafficking in Persons (TIP) Report."

39. "Modern-Day Slavery in Africa: 40,000 Nigerian Women Trafficked for Sex," via *New York Times*, September 10, 2014.

40. Adam Nossiter, "Nigerian Islamist Leader Threatens to Sell Kidnapped Girls," *New York Times*, May 5, 2014, https://www.nytimes.com/2014/05/06/world/africa/nige-ria-kidnapped-girls.html?smid=fb-share&smv1&_r=0.

41. Drew Hinshaw and Joe Parkinson, "The 10,000 Kidnapped Boys of Boko Haram," *Wall Street Journal*, August 12, 2016, https://www. wsj.com/articles/the-kidnapped-boys-of-boko-haram-1471013062.

42. Ibid.

43. Mary Chastain, "Nigeria Raids 'Baby Factory,' Where Pregnant Teens Are Forced to Sell Babies to Foreigners," *Breitbart*, June 16, 2015,

191

http://www.breitbart.com/national-security/2015/06/16/
nigeria-raids-baby-factory-where-pregnant-teens-are-forced-to-
sell-babies-to-foreigners/; "Babies Bred for Sale in Nigeria,"
South Africa Mail & Guardian, November 9, 2008,
http://mg.co.za/article/2008-11-09-babies-bred-for-sale-in-nigeria.

44. US Department of State, Bureau of Democracy, Human Rights, and
Labor, "Country Reports on Human Rights Practices for 2013:
Nigeria," https://www.state.gov/j/drl/rls/hrrpt/2013
humanrightsreport/index.htm?year=2013&dlid=220146.

45. US Department of State, "2016 Trafficking in Persons (TIP) Report."

46. Christabel Ligami, "Presence of Modern-Day Slavery High in
East Africa," *The East African*, November 1, 2013,
http://www.theeastafrican.co.ke/news/Prevalence-of-modern-day-
slavery-high-in-East-Africa-/-/2558/2056232/-/ing6kaz/-/index.html.

47. US Department of State, "2016 Trafficking in Persons (TIP) Report."

48. *Encyclopaedia Brittanica*, s.v. "Zanj Rebellion: Abbasid History."

49. Robert O. Collins, *Eastern African History* (Princeton, NJ:
Markus Wiener Publishers, 1990), p. 54.

50. Ibid., p. 57.

51. Nazer and Lewis, *Slave*, p. 172.

52. "The Arab Muslim Slave Trade of Africans: The Untold Story,"
November 15, 2012, http://originalpeople.org/the-arab-muslim-
slave-trade-of-africans-the-untold-story/.

Chapter Five: Asia

1. Blaine Harden, *Escape from Camp 14: One Man's Remarkable
Odyssey from North Korea to Freedom in the West*
(New York: Viking Penguin, 2012), p. 3.

2. "North Korea Prison Camps 'Like the Holocaust,' Survivors Who
Escaped Say," news.com.au, February 24, 2013, http://www.news.
com.au/world/north-korea-prison-camps-like-the-holocaust-survivors-
who-escaped-say/news-story/53c3f6aabcec81414932c13cc7b5416c.

3. Ibid.

4. Tom Blackwell, "'We Were Slave Owners': Ex-Prison Guard
Taught to View North Korean Inmates as Sub-human 'Enemies,'"
National Post, September 27, 2013, http://news.nationalpost.
com/news/we-were-slave-owners-ex-prison-guard-taught-
to-view-north-korean-inmates-as-sub-human-enemies.

5. Harden, *Escape from Camp 14.*

6. Office of the United Nations High Commissioner for Human Rights (OHCHR), "Report of the Commission of Inquiry on Human Rights in the Democratic People's Republic of Korea"(UN General Assembly, 2014), http://www.ohchr.org/EN/HRBodies/HRC/CoIDPRK/Pages/Re-portoftheCommissionofInquiryDPRK.aspx, accessed February 9, 2014.

7. Harden, *Escape from Camp 14*; US Department of State, Office of the Under Secretary for Civilian Security, Democracy, and Human Rights, "The 2016 Trafficking in Persons (TIP) Report," June 2016, https://www.state.gov/documents/organization/258876.pdf.

8. US Department of State, "2016 Trafficking in Persons (TIP) Report."

9. Office of the United Nations High Commissioner for Human Rights, "Report of the Detailed Findings of the Commission of Inquiry on Human Rights in the Democratic People's Republic of Korea," A/HRC/25/CRP.1, February 7, 2014, https://documents-dds-ny.un.org/doc/UNDOC/GEN/G14/108/71/PDF/G1410871.pdf?OpenElement.

10. Office of the United Nations High Commissioner for Human Rights, "North Korea: UN Commission Documents Wide-Ranging and Ongoing Crimes against Humanity, Urges Referral to ICC," press release, February 17, 2014, http://www.ohchr.org/EN/NewsEvents/Pages/DisplayNews.aspx?NewsID=14255&LangID=E.

11. Steve Hopkins, "Paying Their Debts Back Brick by Brick: The Pakistani Modern Day Slaves Trapped in a Lifetime of Hardship," *UK Daily Mail*, December 3, 2014, http://www.dailymail.co.uk/news/article-2858775/Paying-debts-brick-brick-Pakistani-modern-day-slaves-trapped-lifetime-hardship.html.

12. Alex Rodriguez, "Pakistan Kiln Laborers Hemmed In by Debts They Can't Repay," *Los Angeles Times*, January 9, 2013, http://articles.latimes.com/2013/jan/09/world/la-fg-pakistan-kilns-20130110.

13. National Coalition Against Bonded Labor, "The State of Bonded Labor in Pakistan," 2009, http://socialfilms.weebly.com/uploads/1/9/7/4/19749527/__state-of-bonded-labor-final-final-1-21-07.pdf, p. 32.

14. Juan Campos, "Women in Modern Day Slavery in Pakistan," Borgen Project, March 20, 2014, http://borgenproject.org/women-modern-day-slavery-pakistan/.

15. Annabel Symington, "Life as a Slave in Pakistan," RealClear World, June 3, 2014, http://www.realclearworld.com/articles/2014/06/03/life_as_a_slave_in_pakistan_110555.html.

16. "Selling Children to Pay Off a Debt," IRIN, June 6, 2011, http://www.irinnews.org/feature/2011/06/06/selling-children-pay-debt.

17. Andrew Bushell, "Sale of Children Thrives in Pakistan," *Washington Times*, January 21, 2002, http://www.rawa.org/child-sold.htm.

18. Walk Free Foundation, *The Global Slavery Index 2016* (Perth, Australia: Minderoo Foundation, 2016), http://assets.globalslaveryindex.org/downloads/Global+Slavery+Index+2016.pdf.

19. US Department of State, "2016 Trafficking in Persons (TIP) Report," p. 302.

20. Walk Free Foundation, *The Global Slavery Index 2014* (Claremont: Hope for Children Organization Australia, 2014), http://assets.globalslaveryindex.org/content/uploads/2016/08/30110259/2014-Global-Slavery-Index.pdf., p. 78.

21. Anti-Slavery International, "Fact Sheet: Bonded Labour," http://www.antislavery.org/includes/documents/cm_docs/2009/b/bonded_labour.pdf.

22. Shilpa Kannan, "Child Labour: India's Hidden Shame," *BBC News*, February 5, 2014, http://www.bbc.com/news/business-25947984.

23. Swathi Mehta, "A Report on Debt Bondage, Carpet-Making, and Child Slavery, iAbolish.org, 2010, http://www.iabolish.org/index.php?option=com_content&id=184:a-report-on-debt-bondage-carpet-making-and-child-slavery-&Itemid=8.

24. Ibid.

25. Ibid.

26. Justice P. N. Bhagwati, Indian Supreme Court judge, 1982, quoted in http://www.antislavery.org/includes/documents/cm_docs/2009/b/bonded_labour.pdf.

27. Anti-Slavery International, "Slavery on the High Street: Forced Labour in the Manufacture of Garments for International Brands," June 2012, http://www.antislavery.org/includes/documents/cm_docs/2012/s/1_slavery_on_the_high_street_june_2012_final.pdf.

28. Ibid.

29. Humphrey Hawksley, "Why India's Brick Kiln Workers 'Live Like Slaves,'" *BBC News*, January 2, 2014, http://www.bbc.com/news/world-asia-india-25556965.

30. Ibid.

31. Kannan, "Child Labour: India's Hidden Shame."

32. Anti-Slavery Society, "Child Slaves of South Asia," http://www.anti-slaverysociety.addr.com/slaverysasia.htm.

33. Maggie Black, "Women in Ritual Slavery: *Devadasi, Jogini*, and *Mathamma* in Karnataka and Andhra Pradesh, Southern India," Anti-Slavery International, 2007, http://www.antislavery.org/includes/documents/cm_docs/2009/w/women_in_ritual_slavery2007.pdf.

34. Nash Colundalur, "Devadasis Are a Cursed Community," *The Guardian*, January 21, 2011, https://www.theguardian.com/lifeandstyle/2011/jan/21/devadasi-india-sex-work-religion.

35. US Department of State, "2016 Trafficking in Persons (TIP) Report."

36. Annie Kelly and Mei-Ling McNamara, "A Slave in Scotland: 'I Fell into a Trap—and I Couldn't Get Out,'" *The Guardian*, April 28, 2016, https://www.theguardian.com/global-development/2016/may/28/slavery-human-trafficking-hotel-workers-bangladesh-scotland.

37. Philip Pullella, "Pope Condemns Bangladesh Working Conditions as 'Slave Labor,'" Reuters, May 1, 2013, http://www.reuters.com/article/us-bangladesh-building-pope-idUSBRE9400VT20130501.

38. US Department of State, "2016 Trafficking in Persons (TIP) Report"; Pep Bonet, "Child Labour and Exploitation in Bangladesh," NOOR Foundation, http://noorimages.com/feature/child-labour-and-exploitation-in-bangladesh/.

39. Kate Hodal, Chris Kelly, and Felicity Lawrence, "Revealed: Asian Slave Labour Producing Prawns for Supermarkets in US, UK," *The Guardian*, June 10, 2014, https://www.theguardian.com/global-development/2014/jun/10/supermarket-prawns-thailand-produced-slave-labour?CMP=share_btn_gp.

40. Ibid.

41. Kyla Ryan, "Cambodia's Ongoing Human Trafficking Problem," *The Diplomat*, July 28, 2014, http://thediplomat.com/2014/07/cambodias-ongoing-human-trafficking-problem/.

42. Nisha Varia, "A Victory Against Modern Day Slavery," Human Rights Watch, December 1, 2012, https://www.hrw. org/news/2012/12/01/victory-against-modern-day-slavery.

43. The Arakan Project, "Forced Labour Still Prevails: An Overview of Forced Labour Practices in North Arakan, Burma (November 2011 to May 2012)," http://www.burmalibrary.org/ docs13/AP-Forced_Labour_prevails.pdf.

44. Anwar M. S., "Myanmar Border Police to Resume Nasaka's Oppressive Mechanism against Rohingya," *Rohingya Vision*, June 2, 2014, http://www.rvisiontv.com/myanmar-border-police-resume-nasakas-oppressive-mechanism-rohingya/.

45. Syed Zain Al-Mahmood, "Human Traffickers in Bay of Bengal Cast Sights on Bangladesh," *Wall Street Journal*, October 28, 2014, https://www.wsj.com/articles/human-traffickers-in-bay-of-bengal-cast-sights-on-bangladesh-1414536642.

46. "Myanmar Bans Officials from Saying 'Rohingya,'" Al Jazeera Network, June 21, 2016, http://www.aljazeera.com/news/2016/06/ myanmar-bans-officials-rohingya-160621131628167.html.

47. "Brides for Sale: Trafficked Vietnamese Girls Sold into Marriage in China," *The Guardian*, June 29, 2014), https://www.theguardian.com/global-development/2014/jun/29/ brides-for-sale-trafficked-vietnamese-girls-sold-marriage-china.

48. Pamela Boykoff and Alexandra Field, "Vietnam Girls Smuggled into China and Sold as Child Brides," CNN Freedom Project, April 19, 2016, http://www.cnn.com/2016/04/17/asia/ vietnamese-girls-child-brides-china/index.html.

49. Jesse Sage and Liora Kasten, eds., *Enslaved: True Stories of Modern Day Slavery* (New York: Palgrave Macmillan, 2006), p. 127.

50. *Wall Street Journal*, June 19, 2007, p. 1.

51. *Wall Street Journal*, August 14, 2007.

52. Tiantian Zheng, "China: Sex Work and Human Trafficking (Part 1)," *Fair Observer*, August 19, 2013: http://www.fairobserver.com/ region/asia_pacific/china-sex-work-human-trafficking-part-1/.

53. Saher Khan, "Cotton Farming in Uzbekistan Is 'Modern Slavery,'" Muftah, May 5, 2016, http://muftah.org/cotton-farming-uzbekistan-modern-slavery/.

54. Daniel Sandford, "Trafficking: The Ordeal of a Moscow 'Shop

Slave,'" *BBC News*, November 16, 2012,
http://www.bbc.com/news/world-europe-20338534.

55. Grigory Tumanov, "Russia, Land of Slaves," oDR: Russia and Beyond, November 23, 2012, https://www.opendemocracy.net/od-russia/grigory-tumanov/russia-land-of-slaves.

56. Allison Quinn, "How to Free a Modern-Day Slave in Dagestan," *Moscow Times*, January 15, 2014, https://themoscowtimes.com/news/how-to-free-a-modern-day-slave-in-dagestan-31128.

57. Nikita Aronov, "Russia's Hidden Slave Labor Market," *Russia Beyond the Headlines*, December 5, 2013, http://rbth.com/society/2013/12/05/russias_hidden_slave_labor_market_32307.html.

58. Oxana Vozhdaeva, "Vietnam Workers Kept Like Slaves at Factory in Russia," *BBC News*, August 10, 2012, http://www.bbc.com/news/world-europe-19197095.

Chapter Six: The New World

1. J. M. Cohen, ed. and trans., *The Four Voyages of Christopher Columbus* (London: Penguin Books, 1969), pp. 135–137.

2. Samuel Eliot Morison, *Admiral of the Ocean Sea: A Life of Christopher Columbus* (New York: Book-of-the-Month Club, 1992), p. 342.

3. Ibid., p. 291.

4. Cohen, *Four Voyages of Christopher Columbus*, pp. 58–59.

5. Ibid., p. 122.

6. Morison, *Admiral of the Ocean Sea*, p. 493.

7. David Brion Davis and Steven Mintz, *The Boisterous Sea of Liberty: A Documentary History of America from Discovery through the Civil War* (Oxford: Oxford University Press, 1998), p. 37.

8. Dinkinish O'Connor, "Slavery Survivors Highlight 2015 Broward College–Free the Slaves–ATEST Trafficking Conference," March 30, 2015, http://www.freetheslaves.net/slavery-survivors-highlight-2015-broward-college-fts-atest-trafficking-conference/; Terry Fitzpatrick, "Major Anti-Slavery Organizations Join Forces in Haiti for Greater Impact," Free the Slaves, September 9, 2015, http://www.freetheslaves.net/major-anti-slavery-organizations-join-forces-in-haiti-for-greater-impact/.

9. Corey Adwar, "Why Haiti Is One of the Worst Countries for Child Slavery," *Business Insider*, September 3, 2014,

http://www.businessinsider.com/flawed-arrangement-
turns-haitian-restaveks-into-slaves-2014-8.

10. Free the Slaves, "Slavery in Haiti: The Practice of 'Restavèk,'"
http://www.freetheslaves.net/where-we-work/haiti/;
Andrea Gonzalez-Ramirez, "These Children Are Trapped in
'Modern-Day Slavery,'" *Refinery29*, August 18, 2016,
http://www.refinery29.com/2016/08/120117/modern-day-slavery-
children-haiti-photos#slide.

11. Seymour Drescher and Stanley L. Engerman, eds., *A Historical Guide
to World Slavery* (New York: Oxford University Press, 1998),
pp. 134–137.

12. Free the Slaves, "Where We Work: Haiti," http://www.freetheslaves.
net/where-we-work/haiti/; Adwar, "Why Haiti Is One of the Worst
Countries for Child Slavery"; Abolish Slavery.org, "Haiti,"
http://abolishslavery.org/missions/haiti/.

13. "Black Sugar: Modern-Day Slavery in the Dominican Republic,"
DominicanWatchdog.org, February 4, 2013,
http://www.dominicanwatchdog.org/dominican_news/page-
Black_Sugar_l_Modern-Day_Slavery_in_the_Dominican_Republic.

14. Kadir van Lohuizen, "Slavery on the Sugarcane Plantation,"
NOOR Foundation, http://noorimages.com/feature/slavery-on-the-
sugarcane-plantation/; Judith Garcia, "Sugarcane Slavery in
the Dominican Republic," Spring 2015 SP 100.01 (blog),
https://spring2015sp100.wordpress.com/2015/02/20/
sugarcane-slavery-in-the-dominican-republic/.

15. Jo Tuckman, "Sexual Slavery in Mexico: A Pimp Tells His Story,"
The Guardian, March 3, 2014, https://www.theguardian.com/
global-development/2014/feb/03/sexual-slavery-mexico-pimp-
trafficking-prostitution-story.

16. "Ten Facts on Modern-Day Slavery in Mexico and Haiti,"
The Globalist, February 20, 2015, https://www.theglobalist.
com/10-facts-on-modern-slavery-in-mexico-and-haiti/.

17. Eric Gottwald, "Modern Day Slavery in Mexican Tomato Fields,"
International Labor Rights Forum, December 11, 2014,
http://www.laborrights.org/blog/201412/modern-day-slavery-
mexican-tomato-fields.

18. Bobby Vaughn, "Blacks in Mexico: A Brief Overview,"

Mexconnect, January 1, 2006, http://www.mexconnect. com/articles/1934-blacks-in-mexico-a-brief-overview.

19. Fabíola Ortiz, "Face of Slave Labour Changing in Brazil," Inter Press Service, April 30, 2014, http://www.ipsnews.net/2014/04/face-slave-labour-changing-brazil/.

20. Vincent Bevins, "Brazil Workers Exploited as Modern-Day Amazon Slaves," *Los Angeles Times*, June 7, 2012, http://articles.latimes. com/2012/jun/07/world/la-fg-brazil-slave-labor-20120607.

21. "Update 1: Brazil Convicts Odebrecht Group for Slavery-like Practices in Angola," Reuters, September 1, 2015, http://www.reuters. com/article/brazil-odebrecht-slavery-idUSL1N11802U20150902.

22. Bhavna Sharma, "Contemporary Forms of Slavery in Brazil," Anti-Slavery International, 2006, http://www.antislavery.org/ includes/documents/cm_docs/2009/c/contemporary_forms_ of_slavery_in_brazil.pdf.

Chapter Seven: United States

1. US Department of Justice, Federal Bureau of Investigation, "Operation Cross Country: Recovering Victims of Child Sex Trafficking," Operation Cross Country VIII press conference, June 23, 2014, https://www.fbi.gov/video-repository/ newss-operation-cross-country-viii-press-conference/view.

2. Steve Hargreaves, "I Was a Modern-Day Slave in America," *CNN Money*, November 25, 2013, http://money.cnn. com/2013/11/21/news/economy/human-trafficking-slave/.

3. Holly Austin Smith, *Walking Prey: How America's Youth Are Vulnerable to Sex Slavery* (New York: St. Martin's Press, 2014); http://hollyaustinsmith.com/hollys-story/.

4. Aaron Sankin, "South San Francisco Sex Slavery: Police Bust Shocking Underage Prostitution Ring in Airport Hotel," *Huffington Post*, February 21, 2013, http://www.huffingtonpost.com/2013/02/21/ south-san-francisco-sex-slavery_n_2734350.html.

5. "Park Hills, Mo., Woman Pleads Guilty in Sex-Trafficking Case Involving Teen," *St. Louis Post-Dispatch*, May 12, 2016, http://www.stltoday.com/news/local/crime-and-courts/ park-hills-mo-woman-pleads-guilty-in-sex-trafficking-case/ article_b7a8eefd-06c5-5454-b8ec-d3de9ee58437.html.

6. US Department of Justice, Federal Bureau of Investigation, press releases: "FBI Announces Results of Operation Cross Country X," October 17, 2016, https://www.fbi.gov/news/pressrel/press-releases/fbi-announces-results-of-operation-cross-country-x; "FBI, Partners Complete Operation Cross Country X," October 18, 2016, https://www.fbi.gov/contact-us/field-offices/sanfrancisco/news/press-releases/fbi-partners-complete-operation-cross-country-x.

7. US Department of Justice, Federal Bureau of Investigation, "Justice in Labor Trafficking Case: Subjects Get Lengthy Prison Terms," September 9, 2014, https://www.fbi.gov/news/stories/justice-in-labor-trafficking-case.

8. US Department of Justice, "Tacoma Woman Sentenced for Holding Domestic Servant in Forced Labor," press release, January 28, 2008, https://www.justice.gov/archive/opa/pr/2008/January/08_crt_072.html; Daniela Perdomo, "Couple Sentenced in Forced Labor Case," *Los Angeles Times*, January 29, 2008, p. B5, http://articles.latimes.com/2008/jan/29/local/me-slave29.

9. *U.S. v. Sabhnani*, March 25, 2010; see http://www.leagle.com/decision/In%20FCO%2020100325000T/US%20v.%20SABHNANI.

10. "Nine Charged in Sex Slavery Case in LA," *USA Today*, August 10, 2007, http://usatoday30.usatoday.com/news/nation/2007-08-10-sex-slavery-case_N.htm.

11. US Department of Justice, "Six Indicted in Conspiracy for Trafficking and Holding Migrant Workers in Conditions of Forced Labor in Western New York," press release, June 19, 2002, https://www.justice.gov/archive/opa/pr/2002/June/02_crt_360.htm.

12. "Commerce Clause, 13th Amendment Reviewed in 'Forced Labor' Case (11699)," *New York Daily Record*, January 28, 2004, http://nydailyrecord.com/2004/01/28/commerce-clause-13th-amendment-reviewed-in-forced-labor-case/.

13. Thomas C. Tobin, "For Slavery, Man to Serve Four Years," *St. Petersburg Times*, August 16, 2001.

14. Flor Molina, "'I Was Enslaved for 40 Days,'" The CNN Freedom Project (blog), April 5, 2011, http://thecnnfreedomproject.blogs.cnn.com/2011/04/05/i-was-enslaved-for-40-days/?hpt=C2.

15. Philip D. Curtin, *The Atlantic Slave Trade: A Census* (Madison: University of Wisconsin Press, 1969), pp. 86–93.

16. Harvard University, Hutchins Center for African & American Research, "Trans-Atlantic Slave Trade Database," http://hutchinscenter.fas.harvard.edu/research-projects/projects/trans-atlantic-slave-trade-database.

17. Junius P. Rodriguez, *Slavery in the United States: A Social, Political, and Historical Encyclopedia* (Santa Barbara, CA: ABC-CLIO, 2007), pp. 497–498.

18. Ibid., pp. 3–17.

19. Ibid., p. 87.

20. Ibid., p. 8.

Chapter Eight: Summary

1. *Jones v. Alfred H. Mayer Co.*, 392 US 409 (1968), https://www.law.cornell.edu/supremecourt/text/392/409.

2. Amy O'Neill Richard, "International Trafficking in Women to the United States: A Contemporary Manifestation of Slavery and Organized Crime," Intelligence Monograph, DCI Exceptional Intelligence Analyst Program, Center for the Study of Intelligence, April 2000, https://www.cia.gov/library/center-for-the-study-of-intelligence/csi-publications/books-and-monographs/trafficking.pdf.

3. Free the Slaves and Human Rights Center, University of California, Berkeley, *Hidden Slaves: Forced Labor in the United States*, September 2004, https://www.law.berkeley.edu/files/hiddenslaves_report.pdf, p. 5.

4. Susan Heitler, "The Kidnapped Girls in Nigeria, Modern Slavery, and You," *Psychology Today*, May 16, 2014, https://www.psychologytoday.com/blog/resolution-not-conflict/201405/the-kidnapped-girls-in-nigeria-modern-slavery-and-you.

5. International Labour Organization, "ILO 2012 Global Estimate of Forced Labour Executive Summary" (Geneva: International Labour Organization, ILO Special Action Programme to Combat Forced Labour [SAP-FL], Programme for the Promotion of the Declaration of Fundamental Principles and Rights at Work, 2012), http://www.ilo.org/wcmsp5/groups/public/---ed_norm/---declaration/documents/publication/wcms_181953.pdf.

6. "Modern Slavery 101," iAbolish.org, http://iabolish.org/index.php?option=com_content&view=article&id=25:modern-slavery-101&catid=4:modern-slavery-101&Itemid=7.

7. "Trafficking: Slaves on the Move," iAbolish.org, http://iabolish.org/index.php?option=com_content&view=article&id=183:trafficking-slaves-on-the-move&catid=5:essays-on-slavery&Itemid=8.

8. Kelly E. Hyland, "Protecting Human Victims of Trafficking: An American Framework," *Berkeley Women's Law Journal* 16 (2001): 29, 38–39. "The Twelve Most Profitable International Crimes," 247wallst.com, February 10, 2011.

9. International Labour Organization, "Forced Labour, Modern Slavery, and Human Trafficking," http://www.ilo.org/global/topics/forced-labour/lang--en/index.htm; International Labour Organization, "Profits and Poverty: The Economics of Forced Labour," May 20, 2014, http://www.ilo.org/global/publications/ilo-bookstore/order-online/books/WCMS_243391/lang--en/index.htm; http://www.freetheslaves.org; Meredith May, "Sex Trafficking: San Francisco Is a Major Center for International Crime Networks That Smuggle and Enslave," *San Francisco Chronicle*, October 6, 2006, http://www.sfgate.com/news/article/SEX-TRAFFICKING-San-Francisco-Is-A-Major-Center-2468554.php; Mark Lorey, "Child Soldiers: Care and Protection of Children in Emergencies; A Field Guide," Save the Children Federation, 2001, http://www.savethechildren.org/atf/cf/%79def2ebe-10ae-432c-9bd0-df91d2eba74a%7D/CHILDSOLDIERSFIELDGUIDE.PDF.

10. "Modern Slavery 101," iAbolish.org.

11. The International Labour Organization estimates that 218 million people between the ages of five and seventeen are exploited for their labor, 126 million are in forced labor situations, 74 million work under hazardous conditions, and 8.4 million are in actual slavery. Anti-Slavery International, "Child Labour," http://www.antislavery.org/includes/documents/cm_docs/2009/c/1_child_labour.pdf.

Bibliography

Abbott, Elizabeth. *Sugar: A Bittersweet History.* London: Duckworth Overlook, 2009.

Al-Fasi, Al-Hassan Ibn-Mohammed Al-Wezaz [Leo Africanus, pseud.]. *The History and Description of Africa and of the Notable Things Therein Contained.* Edited by Robert Brown. Translated by John Pory. London: Hakluyt Society, 1896.

Alpers, Edward A. *The East African Slave Trade.* Nairobi: Published for the Historical Association of Tanzania by the East African Pub. House, 1967.

Aristotle. *Politics. Books 1, 2, and 3.* Translated by Benjamin Jowett. N.p.: Classics-Unbound, 2008.

Austen, Ralph A. "The Mediterranean Islamic Slave Trade out of Africa: A Tentative Census." Slavery & Abolition 13.1 (April 1992): 214–248.

———. "The Trans-Saharan Slave Trade: A Tentative Census." In *The Uncommon Market: Essays in the Economic History of the Atlantic Slave Trade,* edited by Henry A. Gemery and Jan S. Hogendorn. New York: Academic Press, 1979.

Bales, Kevin. *Disposable People: New Slavery in the Global Economy.* Rev. ed. Berkeley: University of California Press, 2012.

Bales, Kevin, and Ron Soodalter. *The Slave Next Door: Human Trafficking and Slavery in America Today.* Berkeley: University of California Press, 2009.

Battuta, Ibn. *Travels in Asia and Africa 1325–1354.* Translated and edited by H. A. R. Gibb. London: Broadway House, 1929.

Beachey, R. W. *The Slave Trade of Eastern Africa.* New York: Barnes & Noble Books, 1976.

Bok, Francis. *Escape from Slavery: The True Story of My Ten Years in Captivity and My Journey to Freedom in America.* New York: St. Martin's Press, 2003.

Bradley, K. R. "On the Roman Slave Supply and Slavebreeding." *Slavery & Abolition 8, no. 1* (May 1987): 42–64. Published online June 13, 2008. http://dx.doi.org/10.1080/01440398708574926.

Bradley, Keith. *Slavery and Society at Rome.* Cambridge: Cambridge University Press, 2006.

——. *Slaves and Masters in the Roman Empire: A Study in Social Control*. New York: Oxford University Press, 1987.

Cantor, Norman F. *The Civilization of the Middle Ages*. New York: HarperCollins, 1993.

Cohen, J. M., ed. and trans. *The Four Voyages of Christopher Columbus*. London: Penguin Books, 1969.

Collins, Robert O. *Eastern African History*. Princeton, NJ: Markus Wiener Publishers, 1990.

Crone, Patricia. *Slaves on Horses: the Evolution of the Islamic Polity*. Cambridge: Cambridge University Press, 1980.

Crone, Patricia. *God's Rule: Government and Islam*. New York: Columbia University Press, 2004.

Curtin, Philip D. *The Atlantic Slave Trade: A Census*. Madison: University of Wisconsin Press, 1969.

Davis, David Brion. *Inhuman Bondage: The Rise and Fall of Slavery in the New World*. Oxford: Oxford University Press, 2006.

——. *In the Image of God: Religion, Moral Values, and Our Heritage of Slavery*. New Haven, CT: Yale University Press, 2001.

——. *The Problem of Slavery in the Age of Revolution, 1775–1823*. Rev. ed. New York: Oxford University Press, 1999.

——. *The Problem of Slavery in Western Culture*. New York: Oxford University Press, 1988.

——. *Slavery and Human Progress*. New York: Oxford University Press, 1984.

Davis, David Brion, and Steven Mintz. *The Boisterous Sea of Liberty: A Documentary History of America from Discovery through the Civil War*. Oxford: Oxford University Press, 1998.

Davis, Robert C. *Christian Slaves, Muslim Masters: White Slavery in the Mediterranean, the Barbary Coast, and Italy, 1500–1800*. New York: Palgrave Macmillan, 2003.

Diamond, Jared. *Guns, Germs, and Steel: The Fates of Human Societies*. New York: W. W. Norton & Company, 1999.

Douglass, Frederick. *My Bondage and My Freedom*. Edited by John David Smith. New York: Penguin Books, 2003.

——. *Narrative of the Life of Frederick Douglass, an American Slave, Written by Himself*. Edited by Benjamin Quarles. Cambridge, MA: Harvard University Press, 1960.

Drescher, Seymour. *From Slavery to Freedom: Comparative Studies in the Rise and Fall of Atlantic Slavery.* Basingstoke, U.K.: Macmillan, 1999.

———. *The Mighty Experiment: Free Labor versus Slavery in British Emancipation.* New York: Oxford University Press, 2002.

Drescher, Seymour, and Stanley L. Engerman, eds. *A Historical Guide to World Slavery.* New York: Oxford University Press, 1998.

Durant, Will. *The Story of Civilization. Vol. 2, The Life of Greece.* New York: Simon & Schuster, 1966.

Elkins, Stanley M. *Slavery: A Problem in American Institutional and Intellectual Life.* Chicago: University of Chicago Press, 1959.

Eltis, David. *The Rise of African Slavery in the Americas.* Cambridge: Cambridge University Press, 2000.

Engerman, Stanley L. *Slavery, Emancipation, and Freedom: Comparative Perspectives.* Baton Rouge: Louisiana State University Press, 2007.

———, ed. *Terms of Labor: Slavery, Serfdom, and Free Labor.* Stanford, CA: Stanford University Press, 1999.

Finley, M. I., ed. *Slavery in Classical Antiquity.* Cambridge: Heffer, 1968.

Fogel, Robert William, and Stanley L. Engerman. *Time on the Cross: The Economics of American Negro Slavery.* New York: W. W. Norton & Company, 1989.

———. *The Rise and Fall of American Slavery. Vol. 2, Without Consent or Contract: Conditions of Slave Life and the Transition to Freedom.* New York: W. W. Norton & Company, 1992.

Franklin, John Hope, and Alfred A. Moss Jr. *From Slavery to Freedom: A History of African Americans.* New York: Alfred A. Knopf, 2001.

Fredrickson, George M. *Racism: A Short History.* Princeton, NJ: Princeton University Press, 2002.

Garlan, Yvon. *Slavery in Ancient Greece.* Translated by Janet Lloyd. New York: Cornell University Press, 1988.

Garnsey, Peter. *Ideas of Slavery from Aristotle to Augustine.* Cambridge: Cambridge University Press, 1996.

Genovese, Eugene D. *The Slaveholders' Dilemma: Freedom and Progress in Southern Conservative Thought, 1820–1860.* Columbia: University of South Carolina Press, 1992.

Goldenberg, David. *The Curse of Ham: Race and Slavery in Early Judaism, Christianity, and Islam.* Princeton, NJ: Princeton University Press, 2003.

Gordon, Murray. *Slavery in the Arab World.* New York: New Amsterdam, 1989.

Hall, Shyima, and Lisa Wysocky. *Hidden Girl: The True Story of a Modern-Day Child Slave.* New York: Simon & Schuster BFYR, 2014.

Hanson, Victor Davis. *The Other Greeks: The Family Farm and the Agrarian Roots of Western Civilization.* Berkeley: University of California Press, 1995.

Harden, Blaine. *Escape from Camp 14: One Man's Remarkable Odyssey from North Korea to Freedom in the West.* New York: Viking Penguin, 2012.

Harms, Robert W. *River of Wealth, River of Sorrow: The Central Zaire Basin in the Era of the Slave and Ivory Trade, 1500–1891.* New Haven, CT: Yale University Press, 1981.

Haynes, Stephen R. *Noah's Curse: The Biblical Justification of American Slavery.* New York: Oxford University Press, 2002.

Hellie, Richard. *Slavery in Russia, 1450–1725.* Chicago: University of Chicago Press, 1982.

Hochschild, Adam. *Bury the Chains: Prophets and Rebels in the Fight to Free an Empire's Slaves.* Boston: Houghton Mifflin, 2005.

———. *King Leopold's Ghost: A Story of Greed, Terror, and Heroism in Colonial Africa.* Boston: Houghton Mifflin, 1998.

Homer. *The Iliad.* Translated by Robert Fagles. New York: Viking, 1990.

———. *The Odyssey.* Translated by Robert Fagles. New York: Viking, 1996.

Humphreys, R. Stephen. *Islamic History: A Framework for Inquiry.* Minneapolis: Bibliotheca Islamica, 1988.

Inikori, J. E., ed. *Forced Migration: The Impact of the Export Slave Trade on African Societies.* London: Hutchinson University Library, 1982.

Isaac, Benjamin. *The Invention of Racism in Classical Antiquity.* Princeton, NJ: Princeton University Press, 2004.

Jacobs, Harriet A. *Incidents in the Life of a Slave Girl, Written by Herself.* Cambridge, MA: Harvard University Press, 1987.

Jeal, Tim. *Stanley: The Impossible Life of Africa's Greatest Explorer.* New Haven, CT: Yale University Press, 2007.

Johnson, Walter. *Soul by Soul: Life Inside the Antebellum Slave Market.* Cambridge, MA: Harvard University Press, 1999.

———, ed. *The Chattel Principle: Internal Slave Trades in the Americas.* New Haven, CT: Yale University Press, 2005.

Jones, Howard. *Mutiny on the Amistad: The Saga of a Slave Revolt and Its Impact on American Abolition, Law, and Diplomacy.* New York: Oxford University Press, 1987; rev. ed. 1988.

Josephy, Alvin M. Jr., ed. *The Horizon History of Africa.* New York: American Heritage Publishing, 1971.

Kelek, Necla. *The Foreign Bride: A Report from Inside of Turkish Life in Germany.* Cologne: Kiepenheuer & Witsch, 2005.

Lewis, Bernard. *Islam: From the Prophet Muhammad to the Capture of Constantinople. Vol. 2, Religion and Society.* New York: Oxford University Press, 1974.

———. *Islam in History: Ideas, People, and Events in the Middle East.* London: Alcove Press, 1973.

———. *The Middle East: A Brief History of the Last 2,000 Years.* New York: Scribner, 1995.

———. *The Political Language of Islam.* Chicago: University of Chicago Press, 1988.

———. *Race and Color in Islam.* New York: Octagon Books, 1971.

———. *Race and Slavery in the Middle East: An Historical Enquiry.* New York: Oxford University Press, 1990.

Livingstone, David. *The Last Journals of David Livingstone, in Central Africa, from 1865 to His Death.* Edited by Horace Waller. 2 vols. London: John Murray, 1874.

———. *Missionary Travels and Researches in South Africa.* London: John Murray, 1857.

Livingstone, David, and Henry Morton Stanley. *Life and Finding of Dr. Livingstone: Containing the Original Letters Written by H. M. Stanley, to the "New York Herald."* London: British Library Historical Print Collections, 1874.

Lovejoy, Paul E. *Transformations in Slavery: A History of Slavery in Africa.* 3rd ed. New York: Cambridge University Press, 2012.

———, ed. *The Ideology of Slavery in Africa.* Beverly Hills: Sage Publications, 1981.

MacMichael, Harold Alfred. *A History of the Arabs in the Sudan and Some Account of the People Who Preceded Them and of the Tribes Inhabiting Dárf r.* 2 vols. Cambridge: Cambridge University Press, 1922.

Mandela, Nelson. *Long Walk to Freedom: The Autobiography of Nelson Mandela.* New York: Little, Brown and Company, 1994.

Manning, Patrick. Slavery and African Life: Occidental, Oriental, and African Slave Trades. Cambridge: Cambridge University Press, 2004.

McNeill, William Hardy. *The Rise of the West: A History of the Human Community.* Chicago: University of Chicago Press, 1963.

Mendelsohn, Isaac. *Slavery in the Ancient Near East: A Comparative Study of Slavery in Babylonia, Assyria, Syria, and Palestine, from the Middle of the Third Millennium to the End of the First Millennium.* New York: Oxford University Press, 1949.

Morison, Samuel Eliot. *Admiral of the Ocean Sea: A Life of Christopher Columbus.* New York: Book-of-the-Month Club, 1992.

Nazer, Mende, and Damien Lewis. *Slave: My True Story.* New York: Public Affairs, 2003.

Nihan, James F. *World Slavery: A Documented History.* Laguna Hills, CA: Aegean Park Press, 1999.

Palmié, Stephan, ed. *Slave Cultures and the Cultures of Slavery.* Knoxville: University of Tennessee Press, 1997.

Patterson, Orlando. *Rituals of Blood: Consequences of Slavery in Two American Centuries.* Washington, DC: Civitas/CounterPoint, 1998.

———. *Slavery and Social Death: A Comparative Study.* Cambridge, MA: Harvard University Press, 1982.

Penningroth, Dylan C. *The Claims of Kinfolk: African American Property and Community in the Nineteenth-Century South.* Chapel Hill: University of North Carolina Press, 2003.

Petry, Ann. *Harriet Tubman: Conductor on the Underground Railroad.* New York: HarperCollins, 1983.

Phillips, William D. Jr. *Slavery from Roman Times to the Early Transatlantic Trade.* Minneapolis: University of Minnesota Press, 1985.

Plato. *Collected Works of Plato.* Translated by Benjamin Jowett. New York: Greystone Press, ca. 1930.

Popovic, Alexandre. *The Revolt of African Slaves in Iraq in the Third/Ninth Century.* Translated by Leon King. Princeton, NJ: Markus Wiener Publishers, 1999.

Pulleyblank, E. G. "The Origins and Nature of Chattel Slavery in China." *Journal of the Economic and Social History of the Orient 1*, no. 2

(April 1958): 185–220. http://www.jstor.org/stable/3596015.

Rodriguez, Junius P., ed. *The Historical Encyclopedia of World Slavery.* 2 vols. Santa Barbara, CA: ABC-CLIO, 1999.

———. *Slavery in the United States: A Social, Political, and Historical Encyclopedia.* 2 vols. Santa Barbara, CA: ABC-CLIO, 2007.

Sage, Jesse, and Liora Kasten, eds. *Enslaved: True Stories of Modern Day Slavery.* New York: Palgrave Macmillan, 2006.

Schorsch, Jonathan. *Jews and Blacks in the Early Modern World.* Cambridge: Cambridge University Press, 2004.

Schweinfurth, Georg August. *The Heart of Africa: Three Years' Travels and Adventures in the Unexplored Regions of Central Africa, from 1868 to 1871.* Translated by Ellen E. Frewer. New York: Harper & Brothers, 1874.

Segal, Ronald. *Islam's Black Slaves: The Other Black Diaspora.* New York: Farrar, Straus and Giroux, 2001.

Siculus, Diodorus. *Library of History.* 12 vols. Loeb Classical Library. Cambridge, MA: Harvard University Press, 1933–1967.

Smith, Clarence, and William Gervase. *Islam and the Abolition of Slavery.* New York: Oxford Press, 2006.

Smith, Holly Austin. *Walking Prey: How America's Youth Are Vulnerable to Sex Slavery.* New York: Palgrave Macmillan, 2014.

Snowden, Frank M. Jr. *Blacks in Antiquity: Ethiopians in the Greco-Roman Experience.* Cambridge, MA: Belknap Press of Harvard University Press, 1970.

Tarn, W. W. Hellenistic Civilisation. London: E. Arnold & Company, 1927.

Thomas, Hugh. *The Slave Trade: The Story of the Atlantic Slave Trade, 1440–1870.* New York: Simon & Schuster, 1997.

Thornton, John K. *Africa and Africans in the Making of the Atlantic World, 1440–1800.* Cambridge: Cambridge University Press, 1999.

Toledano, Ehud R. *The Ottoman Slave Trade and Its Suppression, 1840–1890.* Princeton, NJ: Princeton University Press, 1982.

Turner, Richard Brent. *Islam in the African-American Experience. 2nd ed.* Bloomington: Indiana University Press, 2003.

Westermann, William Linn. *The Slave Systems of Greek and Roman Antiquity.* Philadelphia: American Philosophical Society, 1955.

Wiedemann, Thomas. *Greek and Roman Slavery.* London: Routledge, 1994.

Image and Photographic Credits

Page 9: Slave Coffle, Central Africa, 1861; Image Reference C019 as shown on www.slaveryimages.org as compiled by Jerome Handler and Michael Tuite, and sponsored by the Virginia Foundation for the Humanities and the University of Virginia Library. The caption reads "Gang of Captives met at Mbame's on their way to Tette."

The original source of this image was David and Charles Livingstone and was published in *Harper's New Monthly Magazine* (vol.32 [Dec. 1865–May 1866], p. 719).

The image depicts slaves destined for the East African trade with the captive slaves linked by forked logs, children and women attached by chains or ropes, with their African guards armed with guns. This illegal slave trade was well after Great Britain and the United States banned the slave trade in 1808.

Photo section, page 1: Women move bricks. Photograph by Lisa Kristine from *Powerful photos of modern slavery—and survival,* June 26, 2014 (http:ideas.ted.com/images_of_modern_slavery). This photo was taken in India where women balance stacks of bricks on their heads to carry them to nearby trucks. Each brick weighs about six pounds.

Photo section, page 1: Children work in unbearable heat. Photograph taken by Lisa Kristine in Nepal from *Powerful photos of modern slavery—and survival,* Jun 26, 2014 (http:ideas.ted.com/images_of_modern_slavery) Forced child labor in a brick kiln factory in Nepal.

Photo section, page 2: A powerless photographer documenting powerless people. Photograph by Lisa Kristine from *Powerful photos of modern slavery—and survival,* Jun 26, 2014 (http:ideas.ted.com/images_of_modern_slavery).

Kiln workers stacking bricks on their heads to deliver them to their destination. Lisa states that she wanted to break down and cry, but was told there was nothing she could do and she could get them into a worse situation than they were already in.

Photo section, page 2: Brothers Carrying Stone – Nepal. Photograph by Lisa Kristine (http://www.lisakristine.com/portfolio-items/brothers-carry-stone-nepal/?portfolioCats=108 and) *Powerful photos of modern slavery –and survival,* Jun 26, 2014 (http:ideas.ted.com/images_of_modern_slavery)

In this photo taken in the Himalayas, where each day, children make several trips down the mountain, delivering stones from higher up in the Himalayas. They use makeshift harnesses out of ropes and sticks, strapping the stones to their heads and backs. Many of them come from families where everyone is trapped in debt bondage slavery. One of the mothers describes what it was to be in slavery, "Neither can we die, nor can we survive."

Photo section, page 3: Gold in Poisoned Water. Photograph by Lisa Kristine from *Photos That Bear Witness to Modern Slavery*: Lisa Kristine at TED (https://vimeo.com-Free the Slaves, Jan. 23, 2015) and *Powerful photos of modern slavery—and human survival,* June 26, 2014 (http://ideas. ted.com/images_of_modern_slavery)

In the photo, "Slaves pan for gold, wading in water poisoned by mercury used in the extraction process. Children are ever-present, often strapped to the backs of women in the contaminated waters."

Photo section, page 3: A family portrait in toxic color, Blue Red Black-India. Photograph by Lisa Kristine (http://www.lisakristine.com/portfo-lio-items/blue-red-black-india-2-2/?portfolioCats=108) and *Photos That Bear Witness to Modern Slavery: Lisa Kristine at TED (https://vimeo.com-Free the Slaves, Jan. 23, 2015) and Powerful photos of modern slavery—and survival,* June 26, 2014 (http:ted.com/images_of_modern_slavery)

This is a picture that Lisa Kristine took of a textile factory in India, where the dyers are enslaved in a village where each family is involved in a different aspect of making silk. She writes "This is a family portrait. The dyed black hands are the father, while the blue and red hands are his sons. They mix dye in these big barrels, and they submerge the silk into the liquid up to their elbows, but the dye is toxic."

Photo section, page 4: Phuket Town, Thailand – Oct. 13, 2013: Migrant workers on their way to a construction site. Photograph by 1000 Words. Shutterstock.com/modern-day-slavery.

Photo section, page 4: Sulfur miners extracting sulfur inside the crater of Kawah Ijen Volcano in East Java, Indonesia. Very dangerous work in toxic sulfur fumes and fog. Photograph by R. M. Nunes. Shutterstock.com/modern-day-slavery, image no 418466902.

About the Author

W. Kurt Hauser

KURT WAS THE CHIEF ECONOMIST and Chairman of the board of Wentworth, Hauser & Violich (WHV) a San Francisco–based investment management firm. Since 1966, he held positions of Executive Chairman, President, CIO, and CEO at WHV before retiring in 2012. He began his career as an associate, economist, analyst, and portfolio manager at Brundage Story & Rose in New York City.

Kurt was the Chairman of the Board of Overseers of the Hoover Institution from 2001 to 2004. He joined the Board in 1987 and was also the founding Chairman of the Hoover Council between 2008–2013. Kurt continues as a member of the Board of Overseers and the Executive Committee at Hoover. He was a member of the Stanford University Pool C Endowment Investment Committee from 1989 to 2001. He is a member and past president of the Economic Roundtable of San Francisco and was a member of the Association for Investment Management and Research and the Security Analysts of San Francisco.

Kurt is a past chairman of the Alumni Investment Management Committee of the Stanford Business School Trust Fund. He is a past member of the Advisory Board of AON Risk Services. He has served as chairman of the Golden Gate Chapter, American Red Cross; as a board member of the Bay Area Red Cross and The Hill School; and past president and trustee of the Mzuri Wildlife Foundation.

Kurt is the author of *Taxation and Economic Performance* (Hoover Press, 1996). He has authored numerous articles and op/ed pieces and his work has appeared in the *Wall Street Journal*, *The Financial Times*, *Investors Business Daily*, the *Hoover Digest* and *Stanford Magazine*. He has appeared on KRON, CNN, FOX, CNBC, and PJTV. He has also been an invited lecturer for various university, community, trade, and industry groups.

213

Kurt's economic research on the relationship between marginal tax rates, federal government revenues as a percent of Gross Domestic Product (GDP) and economic growth has become known as Hauser's Law.

He received his BA (American History) and MBA degrees from Stanford University (1960 and 1962) and served in the Air National Guard from 1961 to 1967. While at Stanford, Kurt was a member of the varsity track team and rugby team. Kurt is a past member of the Stanford University Athletics Board.

Kurt and his wife, Julianne, reside in Tiburon and Hopland, California; they have four children and nine grandchildren.

Index

215